Bread & Butter the Murders of Polly Frisch

Bread & Butter the Murders of Polly Frisch

Cindy Amrhein
Ellen Lea Bachorski

Polly put the kettle on,
Kettle on, kettle on.
Polly put the kettle on,
We'll all have tea.

Nursery Rhyme
Author unknown

HistorySleuth Publications
2014

Second Edition: Published April 2014

ISBN 978-0-9895533-0-8
HistorySleuth Publications

Cover Image: From the collection of the Wyoming County Historian's office.

First Edition: Published January 16, 2001
First printing: January 2001
Second printing: July 2001

Morris Publishing

Acknowledgements

Many thanks to Sue Conklin, Genesee County Historian; and Don Read, Genesee County Clerk for the excellent job they have done in preserving Genesee County's history.

Special thanks as well to Nancy Maybach Burkard, Jean Brownhill, and Carol Gillette for sharing their family's history; Roger Roeseler for his research at the National Archives on our behalf; Kathy Then for finding Polly the day of her release; and Elena Giorgi and Doris Bannister for their skillful eyes as beta readers in preparations for the revised second edition.

Contents

TABLE OF FIGURES

Foreword

Bread & Butter, a true story of the murders committed by Polly Franklin Hoag Frisch, is the result of extensive research. It began from one paragraph in a book entitled *Gazetteer and Biographical Record and Directory of Genesee County New York 1788-1890,* by F.W. Beers; and the prompting of the Genesee County Historian, Sue Conklin.

Sue felt that Polly's story would be great for the history section of the local monthly paper we published at the time, *The Basom Post.* (Basom is a hamlet of Alabama, NY; Alabama being the scene of where the murders occurred.)

We began researching the story in January of 1995, and quickly came to the conclusion that there was far too much information to put into a news article. It would have to be told in a book.

After reading the story of Polly Frisch, refer back to the following paragraph taken from the Gazetteer mentioned above. It is a fine example of how, after time elapses, the public forgets the facts, details are lost, and the truth becomes folklore.

Cindy Amrhein & Ellen Lea Bachorski

> About the year 1848-1856 Alabama Center was the scene of a crime committed by a woman, Polly Franklin, who married Henry Hoag about 1844. Their children Rosa and Viola, died suddenly, and soon the father died, another child Frances, followed him. After the death of Mr. Hoag his widow married Otto Frisch, but soon was deserted by him.
>
> About this time suspicion was aroused and S.E. Filkins (counselor) caused an investigation to be made, which revealed the fact that some of her family had died from the effects of poison, large quantities of arsenic having been administered to them. She was arrested and tried three times, and being finally found guilty was sentenced to be hung, but was eventually imprisoned for life.

Foreword

Introduction

In 1844 in the small farming town of Alabama, Genesee County, New York, Henry Hoag married Polly Franklin. Polly was 19-years-old, and Henry, 27. Marriage was a natural course of events in the 1800s and divorce was almost unheard of. People married for life unless one spouse died, and children were an expected part of this union.

Female children, if we follow the thinking of the times, held their place only in the household and helping to care for their younger siblings. Male children guaranteed the continuation of the family name. Boys were put to work at a very young age to help with the many tasks involved in the up-keep of a farm. They were taught to handle and care for the livestock as well as planting, cultivating and harvesting the crops. This was a must, as the son(s) would take over the farm when the time was right.

Birth control, as we know it, was not practiced aside from abstinence and families with more than five children were common. Polly would soon come to grips with this reality and she would not like it. Whatever expectations or illusions she held when she first married Henry would disappear with the birth of her first child.

Albert was born on November 15, 1846. For reasons we will never know, unless it was an expression of Polly's feelings, Albert's middle name would be given as "Burden." There is no record of Polly giving birth to any children in the first two years of her marriage. We know the problem was not one of fertility. As soon as Polly gave birth to one child, she was pregnant with another. Over a period of 10 years Polly was pregnant with eight children. Only two would survive in the end.

With the death of her husband and two of her children the town became suspicious that something odd was going on in the Hoag household. After four months of investigation, Polly would be indicted on three counts of murder in the first degree. What would come to light over the next two years would shock and horrify this small knit community to such an extreme that it would haunt them for decades to come.

Polly was not your typical woman of the 1850s. The *Progressive Batavian*, the *Republican Advocate, Genesee Democrat* and the *Genesee County Herald & Spirit of the Times*, all Genesee County's newspapers, had described Polly as "not living in a manner that becomes a woman. Her language was imprudent. She possessed an impassive countenance, and was a woman of great self-control and determination." It was said that Polly was, "...youthful and unprepossessing in appearance. She was five foot tall, small and delicate in stature, with black eyes, a Jewish nose, and a thin and compressed lip."

During her arraignment in November of 1857 the *Genesee Democrat* newspaper stated that, "She exhibited no anxiety, fear or terror, and was apparently as calm in her feelings as a summer morning. She does not appear to realize her awful position, and shows no symptoms of remorse or guilt; but seems to take the proceedings as a trifle matter, and only seemed a little annoyed at the gaze of the multitude."

During Polly's trials, "Her manner was composed and eminently well calculated to impress a casual observer favorably," wrote the *Genesee County Herald & Spirit of the Times*. "She maintained a placidity of demeanor unusual to those on trial for murder, and her exhibition of nerve is almost unparalleled in criminal history," cited the *Genesee Democrat*.

Given these descriptions of Polly's personality, newspaper accounts of the trial testimony from her friends and neighbors, court documents, and other facts found throughout our research we came to three possible conclusions.

When we first started, our thought was that Polly was innocent. There was no solid proof that Polly committed these crimes. In fact, several people helped Polly with the care of her family, almost twenty-four hours a day, during their sickness. Since none of these people stood there and watched Polly put what they thought was arsenic in the food and drink of her husband and children, than how could she possibly accomplish poisoning them? How could she do it and not get caught with others constantly around her? Polly seemed so attentive to her husband, and all would attest to that whether they testified for or against her.

An autopsy proved there was arsenic in the bodies of her dead family members, but arsenic was commonly used for medicinal purposes during the 1800s. Could Polly or the doctors have done it accidentally with one of the medications prescribed? Or, if the Hoag's were intentionally poisoned, could someone other than Polly be responsible? There were a number of contradictory statements in testimony that led us to wonder if it had been someone else.

In an article printed by the *Republican Advocate*, November 17, 1857, Polly claimed—that "she was innocent of this [meaning her family's deaths] or any like offense, and attributed the prosecution to local excitement and prejudice." From this statement it seems obvious she knew that the residents of Alabama didn't like her or her unbecoming behavior. Maybe Polly's calm exterior during the trials was because she knew she was innocent and thought justice would prevail. Did she do it or was the community trying to railroad her out of town? It wasn't until we came across a certain newspaper article and scrutinized court documents that we felt Polly was guilty in some form.

Our next thought was that Polly suffered from an ailment realized only in our era as Munchausen

Syndrome by Proxy. It is a disorder by which a person deliberately makes someone they care for sick. A parent or caregiver creates physical symptoms by giving various medicines. Most of these victims are children, the mother usually being responsible for creating the illness. Hurting the child is not the ultimate goal. The victim is merely the vessel used to gain sympathy from others and keep themself as the focus of everyone's attention. Unfortunately, children have died from this. If this were the case, Polly would have been quite pleased from all the attention received at the numerous trials. She was the focus of attention for over two years.

We feel sure, to an extent, that Polly Frisch had some sort of mental illness. She showed no emotion when she was brought into trial, and was often smiling. Polly just didn't comprehend what was going on and what it would mean if she were convicted. She didn't seem to possess the mental reasoning to distinguish the difference between right and wrong or understand the reason why what she did was not acceptable.

Our final conclusion was that Polly suffered from a combination of a deranged mind and an obsession with someone she couldn't have. Polly was tired of her life and being tied down to her family. She wanted out of the situation to do as she pleased. Town's people had said she was having an affair with another man and that he apparently did not care for children. She wanted him, not her husband Henry, and that was that. It has been seen in modern crimes of passion, that a woman has killed her children over an obsession for a man.

If this was her feeling, then Henry and the children would have to go. Based on all that we know about the events surrounding the deaths, and Polly's personality, we feel that she was the type to do whatever it would take, without a thought as to right or wrong, to get what she wanted—which is exactly what we believe Polly Frisch did.

1

BACKGROUND

In May of 1833, Polly's parents, Schubel and Eliza Franklin, moved the family from Fort Ann in Washington County, NY to the town of Alabama. Schubel purchased a one-quarter acre of land for $60, one and a half miles east of Alabama Center. Eight-year-old Polly and her siblings—Jane, age twelve; Frederick who was ten; William, age three; and Emily who was born two years later—lived here until Schubel purchased the farm north of the Center in Alabama. Along with them came Polly's half sister from Schubel's first marriage, Elizabeth, who was twenty. Elizabeth would marry a local lad named Francis Lamb in 1839.

In October of 1840, Schubel decided to go into farming, and bought 159 acres of land two miles northwest of Alabama Center on what is now called Casey Road. Here he built a barn and a small house. One month later, on November 8, the last of Eliza Franklin gave birth to her last child. They named her Julia. Julia would turn out to be the most avid defender of Polly's innocence.

In 1849 Schubel Franklin bought the property in the town of Alabama which was to be their main residence. The Franklin house was built near the southwest corner of Alabama Center. Right next to the house, on the west side, Schubel built a smaller structure to locate his business. Schubel was a blacksmith by trade.

Alabama, originally called Gerrysville, was created on April 17, 1826 from the north part of the town of Pembroke, and the southern part of the town of Shelby, in Orleans County. In 1828 the town's name was changed to Alabama which means, "Here we rest."

Alabama has four Hamlets: Alabama Center, on the corner where Lewiston and Alleghany Road (called State Road) intersect; South Alabama (also known as Smithville) which lies southeast of the Center; Wheatville, located two and a half miles east of the Center on Lewiston Road; and Basom which wasn't formed until 1889, south of Alabama Center on Alleghany Road.

During the 1800s and early 1900s there was also an area called West Alabama. It was the earliest settlement, in the northwest corner of the town, where Meadville and Lewiston roads intersect. James Walsworth, Alabama's first settler in 1806, turned his home into a tavern in 1808. It was considered the halfway point between the towns of Lewiston and Batavia. Travelers stopped here over night on their way to Batavia to file their deeds. During the 1850s, Valentine Reynolds owned the tavern. Mrs. Reynolds could never have predicted that one day she would testify about the murders committed by a neighboring town's person.

Each Hamlet was a self-sustaining community in a centralized condensed area, usually on four corners of two intersecting main roads. All contained one or more blacksmith and harness shops, tanner and currier, general store, post office, hotel, gun shop, mill, produce store, and of course a house of worship.

The further one traveled from the center of these hamlets, the less populated the area became, thinning out until only vast areas of farmland were visible. Dairy cows and sheep were the main livestock. Chickens were raised for their eggs as well as their meat. Crops of wheat, corn, barley, oats, potatoes, and beans took over the large expanse of open land. Orchards of apples, pears, peaches, and grapes were the primary fruit grown. Goods were shipped to other areas of the country, or sold to the town's produce company which in turn would sell it to the local inhabitants. These were the main source of income along with the production of lumber.

The lumberyards were generally on the outskirts of the center of town located near a river or stream, as the power for the mill was supplied by water. They provided the lumber for home building throughout the towns. The product was also sold to other sections of the country.

Aside from one's own buggy, a horse-drawn stagecoach provided transportation from Alabama Center. The stage line delivered mail, goods, and passengers, to two major locations. Running daily, round trip, the stage traveled from Alabama Center east to Batavia, and north from the Center to Medina. From Batavia, transfers were made via the railroad. Medina's transports continued by way of the Erie Canal.

Several one or two room schoolhouses were located throughout each town in Genesee County to provide easy access. Alabama had fifteen such schools. Schoolhouse #2, built in 1850, was east of Alabama Center. Julia and Emily Franklin might have been educated there. The 1850 census indicated they were in school. It would have been the closest one to their home in Alabama Center. The Alabama Museum has records for some of the schoolhouses, but unfortunately not for #2.

Schoolhouse #3, located up near the farm at the intersection of Casey and Lewiston Roads, was not built until after 1854. It is unknown at which residence the younger Franklin girls lived the majority of the time or which school they attended.

There also are indications that at different points in time Schubel had rented his farm to others. Where they lived in their early years is irrelevant; by 1856, when the murders begin, it becomes important. It not only helps the reader to place the characters in their proper places;

it also serves to show the part the two locations played in the planning and the motive for the crimes.

Henry Hoag purchased his first parcel of land in Alabama in 1844 from his Uncle James Filkins, brother of Henry's mother, Hannah Filkins Hoag. Henry built their home near the southeast corner of Alabama Center on Lewiston Road. He was a shoemaker by trade, and held his shop a short distance from their house. Henry had bought other pieces of land at the Center but soon resold them.

After the Hoag's first child Albert was born, in November of 1846, Polly became pregnant with her first daughter, Roselphe A., who was born in August of the following year. Polly immediately became pregnant again and gave birth to her third child Leonard in May of 1848. Neither Roselphe nor Leonard would live very long. On July 29, at only nine weeks old, Leonard J. Hoag would die. In less than three weeks time, on August 16, Roselphe died as well. They are buried in the same grave together in the Alabama Cemetery, north of the Center.

In March of 1849, Henry Hoag purchased the property directly west of the house where they were presently living. On July 23, Polly gave birth to her fourth child. The Hoags named her Rosalie. The new Hoag home was completed in the early part of 1850. Henry and Polly sold the other house and moved their family next door.

That same year, on the 21st of September, Polly bore a child again. She would be named Frances. Viola, her sixth child, would be born in May of 1852; alas, her life too would be short lived. Viola died at six months on the 8th of November. One would have to wonder if any of her children were colicky. Were the children who lived good babies that gave Polly no problems, or was it just by chance and the illnesses of the times that caused the others to die?

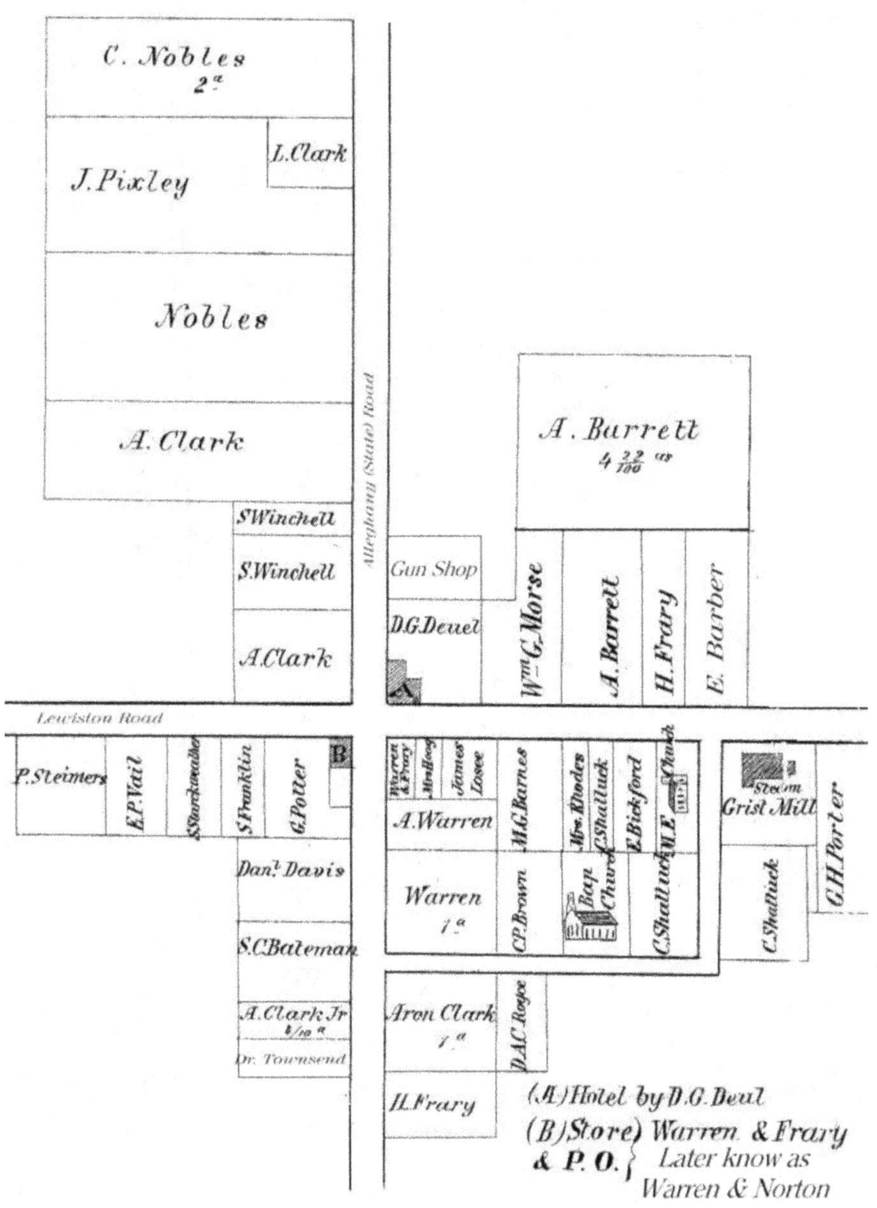

Figure 1. Alabama Center, 1850s.

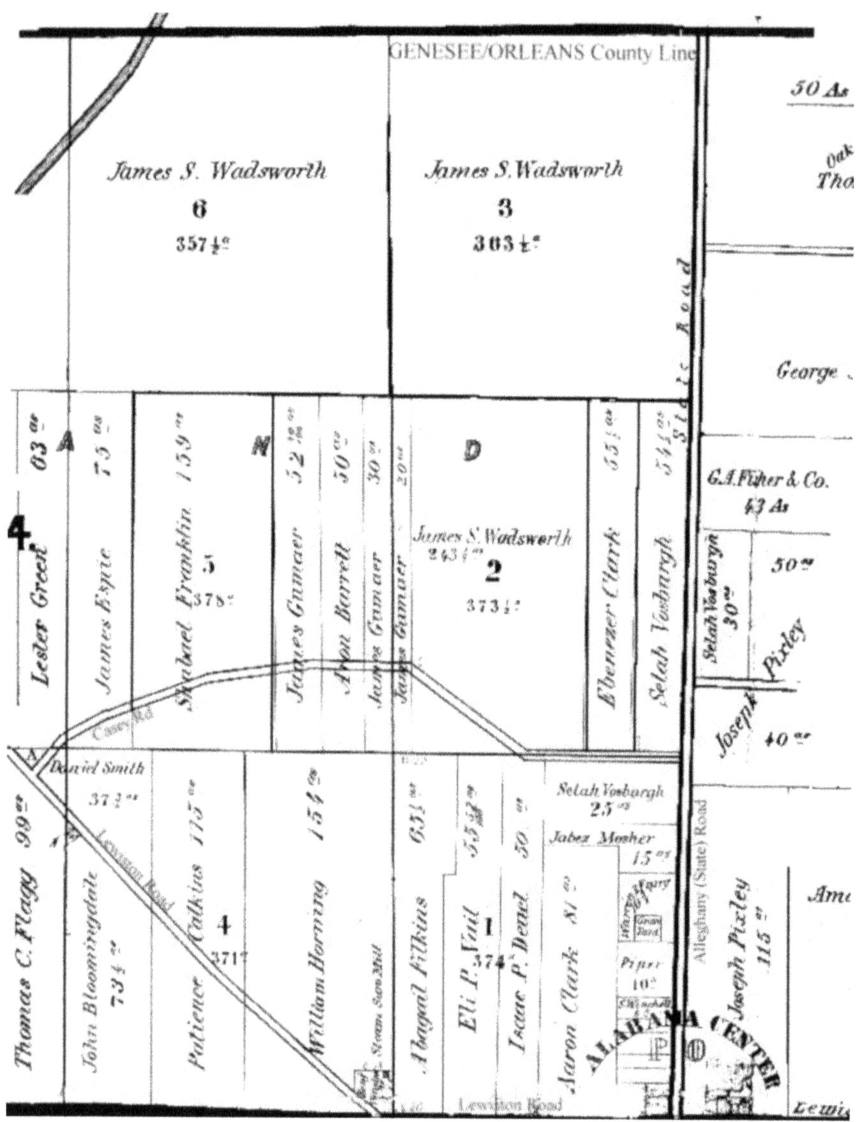

Figure 2. Alabama - Part of the northwest portion of town.

Unfortunately, not much is known about the deaths of the first few children. It was taken for granted that the Hoag children had died due to one of the common diseases of that era such as influenza, scarlet fever, measles, smallpox, dysentery, or diarrhea. No one had suspected foul play until years later. Remember that this was the middle of the 1800s. It was an unthinkable thing that a mother would murder her children; her husband maybe, but not her children.

Life was much harder on women back then. Their responsibilities were many. It must have been very stressful, both mentally and physically, for a young mother to have so many little children very close in age to tend to along with the other duties of running a household. A woman also had few rights in the eyes of the public—even fewer in the eyes of her husband.

It was a woman's duty to honor and obey her spouse at all times, and of course, this included in the bedroom. Judging by the accounts of Polly's attitude, subservient life was not to her liking. Tending to the needs of her husband and children, cleaning, cooking, laundry, and mending were done without the conveniences we now take for granted. They had no electricity, no running water apart from what she pumped from the well, and only a wash board and bucket to clean the clothes of her family.

The Hoags also had sheep, a spinning wheel, and a loom, as stated in Henry's estate papers of what Polly was allowed to keep after his death. It is logical to assume that Polly must have made some of the clothing for her family. This was not a rosy life for Polly, and maybe one day, she decided she had had enough.

By autumn of 1855, Polly and Henry had three children, and one on the way with a due date in January. Henry still had his shoe business, and working with him, an apprentice named Matthew Bardwell. Matthew lived in the same house as the Hoags and was treated as one of the family. He must have been a trusted friend for Henry to allow him to reside in his home and run his business during his absence.

It was a town election year and voting was also a time for social gathering. On November 12th after the men voted, the Hoags went over to the Alabama Hotel for the get-together. The hotel was directly across from the Hoag's house. Miss Mary Orton, a niece of Aaron Clark, and her mother were there visiting from Illinois. In the last seven years the occult and spiritualism had become quite popular due to the Fox sisters from Wayne County, New York, and their claim to be able to communicate with the dead. Miss Orton, a believer, practiced fortune telling, and did so with several of the guests at the Alabama Hotel that night. One of the guests was Polly.

Miss Orton informed Polly that she would leave Alabama Center, and if she did she would lose her husband and child the same year. Julia, Polly's sister, thought Polly had taken the fortune as a joke. But what if she hadn't? Did Polly take this as a serious fact as some people did at the time, or could it have sparked her mind to plan Henry's demise? Polly would refer to her fortune often in future conversations.

Oddly enough, Henry would become very sick that winter and was diagnosed by Dr. Townsend, from Alabama Center, as having a disease called cholera morbus from eating a bad piece of mincemeat pie.

Mincemeat pie, in a recipe from Polly's era, was described as made from scraggy beef, usually a neckpiece, beef suet, cooked and left to stand overnight. Apples, raisins, and spices were added. The ingredients were put in jars, covered with molasses, and sealed tightly for later use. Shelf life was supposedly two months. Considering the ingredients and the way it was stored, it could have caused a number of different ailments created by bacteria.

Along with the surge of immigrants that came to the United States in the early 1800s, came the highly contagious cholera. Immigrants who were already infected carried the disease with them across the ocean to our shores. In the 1840s and 1850s there were several outbreaks in New York State striking the heavy populated areas the worst.

During this time the medical community thought that cholera was contracted from eating unripened fruit, drinking rancid water, or sour liquids. Cholera morbus was the strain that normally came on in the heat of summer. That idea is partially correct. Bacteria reproduce quicker in the heat. It wasn't the food and water itself, but the contamination of them that was the problem. Rats were the biggest carriers of the disease. The Hoags had admitted to a problem with rats. If rats scurried through the flour bins or cupboards carrying the disease, their droppings would infect the food. It would not be discovered until 1883 by bacteriologist Robert Koch, that cholera was a strain of bacteria carried by the victims. It was transferred through the infected victims' feces, urine, or vomit.

So was it botulism, food poisoning, cholera, or something else that made Henry so ill that winter? It was never mentioned that anyone else in the family had gotten sick. Was Henry the only one who ate the pie or was Polly already poisoning him? We have found no historical evidence to show that there was ever a cholera epidemic in the town of Alabama.

The doctors could have easily mistaken the symptoms of arsenic poisoning with that of cholera. Although the symptoms are the same to an extent, it's the differences the doctors didn't pick up on. We must remember that doctors' medical knowledge was limited to what was known in the time period in which they lived. It would have been an easy mistake to make on first observation. They also would have no reason to suspect poison.

Cholera comes on suddenly with the first symptoms appearing one to five days after initial contact. Diarrhea and vomiting occur frequently causing intense pain in the stomach. Even though the body is rapidly losing fluid, the urge to stool and vomit continues. The loss of fluid and dehydration causes death within hours.

Arsenic poisoning involves the same intensity of vomiting and diarrhea, and the same pain in the pit of the stomach due to the continual spasms of the stomach muscles. Depending on the size of the dose, and how often they were administered, a person can be poisoned over a long period of time.

Acute poisoning will show more severe symptoms. The vomit may become tinged with blood. The throat and mouth will begin to burn and feel swollen. Seizures as well as muscle spasms will be evident. The skin may discolor in areas due to disruption in blood flow to arteries. Although the body temperature may be low, the victim will sweat profusely. Eventually they will become delirious, exhausted, and die.

There is no information on Henry's first sickness that winter of 1855. We have no way of knowing what his symptoms were or how he was treated for his illness. Henry and his family were still living in Alabama Center in November of that year, making the doctors easily accessible. Dr. Townsend and Dr. Bateman were on the west side of State Road, a short distance south of the Center. Dr. Nelson Horning lived east in the hamlet of Smithville, now called South Alabama.

Later it will become relevant as to where everyone lived. When Henry succumbed to his final illness, his life slipping away, the time it took the doctors and friends to travel the distance to reach him became vital.

Exactly on the southwest corner of Alabama Center was the general store, first known as Warren & Farley and later, Warren & Norton. General stores at this time carried a variety of goods for every aspect of life. Inside the general store was the post office. Selah Vosburg was the postmaster and also a real estate assessor. Ruben Warren, the deputy postmaster who ran the office a good deal of the time, was also the co-owner of the store.

To the west of the store lived the Potter Family; west of them, Polly's parents, the Franklins, and Julia, Polly's sister. The rest of Polly's siblings were now married and living on their own. Elizabeth, now on her second husband, was married to George Lester. Lester had moved to Alabama from Wyoming County, New York.

Traveling west on the other side of the road from the Franklin house lived the now widowed Abigail Filkins and her children. One of Abigail's sons, Stanley, had studied law in Austinburg, Ohio. He returned to Genesee County after graduating and held a position with the legal team of Brown & Glowacki in Batavia.

In 1857, twenty-one year old Stanley would be admitted to the Bar. As it would turn out, Stanley would be the one to force the investigation of Polly and the murders. After all, he was Henry's cousin, so it is only natural that he would do what he could to make sure that justice was served and Polly was punished.

Schubel Franklin's sister Sarah, and her husband Henry Noble, lived north of the Center; Selah Vosburg north of the Nobles.

Down the road to the east of the Hoags resided Eli Bickford. Eli was also a shoemaker by trade. Directly across the road from Eli lived Mrs. Eliza Barber, a widow, and a friend of the Hoag family.

This is quite a cast of characters to be sure, but all played a role in one form or another in the complex series of events that were about to unfold over the next few months.

2

THE MOVE

In the spring of 1856, after recovering from his illness, Henry decided to give up shoemaking and try his hand at farming. Henry made a deal with Polly's father Schubel to rent his farm for three years. He made a deal with Eli Bickford, another shoemaker, to take over the shoe shop in his absence. This move was a very sore subject between Polly and Henry, and the cause of many heated arguments.

Perhaps in the beginning Henry desired to feel the soil beneath his feet, or maybe it was the sense of accomplishment in reaping a harvest he had grown that prompted his decision to move to the farm. Living in the country would also give Polly and Henry a good deal of privacy. This is something that was unavailable at Alabama Center, where everyone knew everyone else's business and gossip abounded. There were also a lot of people there that didn't care for Polly, and Henry knew it. In the end, Henry's desire to leave the Center would be based on reasons he would have never imagined.

Polly told several people she did not want to leave Alabama Center because of loneliness, and the fear of sickness. It is understandable Polly would be lonely and so would her children. After all, Polly did have some friends there, and most likely, so did her young ones. To move would mean the children would no longer be kept busy by playing with others close by. Polly would also lose her socializing with the ladies of the town whom she had spoken to on a daily basis—at least the ones she got along with.

Figure 3. Former Hoag house. Alabama Center, NY.

Photo by C. Amrhein.

It makes sense that a woman would worry about what would happen if someone in the family became sick. Far away from the town center, the timely availability of a doctor and the quick access to medicine would be much more difficult to acquire in case of an accident or illness.

Polly told Mrs. Barber, as well as others, that if Henry moved upon the farm he would never move off. She mentioned the fortune that was told to her by Miss Orton, that there would be two deaths in the family, and she was not to be one of the two to die.

Although these were the feelings that Polly expressed to others, they were not her true reasons for protesting to the move. Something was going on in Polly's life that was yet to be discovered. Moving to the farm would spoil everything for her. The move was inevitable, and the isolation would turn out to work to Polly's advantage.

As time passed, Polly's hostility towards moving to the farm increased. Mrs. Potter testified during one of the trials that Polly had told her and another woman, Delia Avery, that she was sorry she ever got married. Polly also relayed to the women that she wished she was clear of her husband and children; that she did not care how she got clear of them, nor how soon; and that if it was not for them, she could go anywhere she had a mind to. Polly told the ladies that she would not care a bit if Henry should die. If he moved on the farm, as he was not healthy, he wouldn't live six months.

The moving day was planned for the end of April. The closer April came the more adamantly Polly protested. In her own words she told numerous neighbors, friends, and relatives of her strong objections to the move.

Was this only a wife's anger derived from frustration with a stubborn husband who would not listen to his wife's wishes? Doubtful. Polly's objections were totally selfish and had nothing to do with the needs of her family.

Demeaning her husband and his wishes so blatantly in front of neighbors was an unheard of thing for a woman to do. Polly might have thought that if she complained enough in front of others, Henry would change his mind. Possibly, her complaints to others over her alleged concern for Henry's health were part of her plan. After she murdered Henry she would be able to say to everyone she voiced her objections to, "There, I told everyone that this would happen!"

The Hoags owned a horse and buggy and they were only relocating a mile and a half from the center of town. The distance isn't really that far for normal daily activity. Why was Polly protesting so much? Henry would not find out the real reason until right before the move. The answer would not come from Polly, but from her nine-year-old son Albert.

Aside from the constant arguing, there were other problems in the Hoag's marriage. It was no secret that Henry and Polly were not having sexual relations. Polly had told this to her brother-in-law George Lester. Henry probably assumed their lack of lovemaking was because she had just given birth to Eliza Jane in January. He might have also thought that Polly was worried about getting pregnant right away again. There were already four children to care for as it was. Given the housework, child care, and his working long hours, perhaps Henry thought it was due to lack of time or one of them being tired. Henry was no doubt confused as to Polly's behavior, that is, until Albert told.

One afternoon in early spring, while still living in Alabama Center, Albert walked into the kitchen of the house and viewed a scene that would forever change his opinion of his mother.

Albert's father was over in the shoe shop working. Rosalie, Frances, and a girl who was visiting named Adelaide were not in the house at the time—just the baby Eliza Jane. The bedroom, which was shared by the whole family, was off of the kitchen. It was warm outside so the bedroom door was open. On the bed lying next to his mother was his father's apprentice, Matthew Bardwell.

Albert being the oldest, and only son, was the man of the house during his father's absence. He looked after the children and tried to help his mother take care of everything in the best way a nine-year-old could. They were a family, and it was his responsibility to take care of the others. To see his mother being unfaithful to his father must have been distressing as well as confusing to a young boy. One can only guess what was going through Albert's mind after seeing his parents argue constantly about the move, and now this. He was certainly old enough to understand what his mother and Matthew were doing. Albert did the only thing he could—he went to find his father.

Albert went over to the shoe shop and told everything he had seen. Of all the reasons for Polly objecting to the move, Henry probably never suspected his wife of being unfaithful with his apprentice. No wonder Polly did not want to leave the Center, rent the shoe shop to Eli Bickford, or move to the farm. It would have separated Polly from her lover.

Henry immediately went over to the house and headed directly for the bedroom. Albert followed. Matthew was lying on the outside of the bed, with Polly lying down on the other side of him. Henry had a few words for Matthew and left the room and went back over to the shop. Polly and Matthew were still in bed together when Albert and his father left.

After Henry and his son left the house, Matthew went over to the shoe shop. Henry confronted him as soon as he came in. He made it clear to Matthew that he wanted him to leave his home, but for some reason, the threat was not enforced. Maybe Matthew talked his way out of it. Possibly Henry gave him a "don't let it happen again" ultimatum. For whatever reason, Matthew was allowed to stay, and to continue to work in the shoe shop and board in their home.

With the truth out in the open now, tension was growing between Henry and Polly. Henry's brother Timothy, while on a visit from Michigan, had witnessed an argument between Polly and Henry before the move to the farm. Timothy stated that Polly said she would never go there. Henry responded by threatening that he would go and take the children with him, but did not care if she went or not. Polly in turn told Henry if he did, she would not go, claiming if she could not get away in any other manner she would kill him and would go back to the shoe shop and have Matthew in the shop.

It was getting closer to the end of April and the move to the farm was to become a reality. Henry, off on a trip to Medina, had no idea what was going on at home while he was gone. The weather was getting much warmer now. Albert had gone into the house, possibly for a nap, because once again he headed for the bedroom.

This time the bedroom door was closed, cutting off the breeze that would normally flow through the kitchen door. Albert opened the door to enter the room and found the reason for the door being closed. There was his mother, once again, lying in bed with Matthew Bardwell. The three of them locked eyes for a moment. The two in bed said nothing to Albert nor he to them. Albert left the room and awaited his father's return.

That night when Henry returned from Medina, Albert told his father what had occurred. Matthew had not gone to work that whole day and was in bed when Henry got in. For some reason, Matthew was again allowed to continue to work in the shop; but Albert had never heard his father speak to Matthew again. Henry might have resolved himself to the fact that the only way to get his wife away from Matthew was to get her out of Alabama Center.

On April 23rd, the Hoags moved one and a half miles north to the farm. Julia, Polly's younger sister who visited often, helped them move. Julia was very close to her sister and spent a great deal of time at the Hoag house before she married and moved to Lancaster—more so than at her father's house. Eli Bickford took over Henry's shoe shop. Matthew Bardwell moved to Wheatville, five miles to the east of the Center and presumably worked with one of the tradesmen holding a business there.

From what we can gather from testimony, this ended the relationship on Matthew's part. It was doubtful he had any serious interest in Polly. Aside from the fact she was married, town's people said that he didn't care for children. We don't think this was due to his not liking children in general, but only that he didn't care for having Polly's children around.

In 1856 Polly was a 31-year-old woman with four children ranging from six months to nine years old. Matthew was only 22. It is hard to imagine he would take this relationship seriously, but Polly did. Polly had an aggressive personality and was only interested in what she wanted. We feel Matthew purposely made the distance between them farther in order to get away from her. Matthew eventually took up with a local girl.

For Polly it was not over. She was obsessed with getting Matthew Bardwell back. She continued to try and contact him. Albert had gone in the buggy with Polly one day, thinking they were going to Alabama Center. Instead she rode to Wheatville to see Matthew. Polly and Matthew had a private conversation and then she left with her son. On the way back home to the farm Polly told Albert not to tell his father where she had been.

Polly was discontented. Not only was she away from her friends and her lover, she was separated from all of the conveniences of life. She continued to voice her hatred for farm life.

Polly's brother-in-law George Lester later testified, "I was at the farm house after they moved there in the spring. [I] talked with her when on the farm about staying there. She said she would go back to the Center in the fall, that she did not like staying there [meaning the farm]. She said she did not think Henry would stay there more than a year. Said she hadn't slept with her husband in four months, and that she never would again."

THE MOVE

Farm life must have agreed with Henry, as all had said his health was improving since he moved there. More than likely he felt secure thinking that his wife was separated from her lover. The Hoags raised sheep, dairy cows, and swine according to Henry's probate file. In the acreage that wasn't used for grazing Henry had planted corn. It was Albert's responsibility to help his father with the many daily chores. Polly's father Schubel and her sister Julia were often over to lend the Hoags a hand.

Schubel and his daughters, Julia and Polly, were very close. It is hard to tell whether Schubel and Julia's account of Polly's actions were truth or alibis derived from their devotion to her. Did they think she was innocent or were they protecting her?

Albert on the other hand was highly suspicious of his mother's movements and intentions. The testimonies of Schubel, Julia, and Albert contradicted each other throughout the trials. One thing is certain—at the end of May, Polly went to Dr. Samuel Bateman who was also a druggist, and purchased a half-ounce vial of arsenic. It seems, according to Polly, that the Hoags were having a problem with rats.

Dr. Bateman said, "I got out a half ounce vial near full, labeled 'Arsenic Poison'. She had not got any arsenic from me before. She did not wish to charge it, said she would pay for it in a few days." The reason she didn't want to charge it was to leave no written record that she had purchased it. Polly was not finished yet. She returned a couple weeks later to the Batemans to replenish her supply.

Calista, the doctor's wife, said, "Polly came to my house early one morning in June, she wanted to get into the office to purchase some rhubarb, and some arsenic to kill rats or mice who were destroying her clothes and bedding. She said she had some in the house before, but had mislaid or lost it. She was going to mix it with some bread and butter and put it between the lath. She said her husband did not wish her to buy it, for fear of accident. Said the mice were so thick that she couldn't live in the house. She said rat exterminator did not have any effect when they had used it." Calista continued, "I put up a half an ounce of rhubarb for her at the same time I gave her a small vial of arsenic. I inquired to the health of her family."

Mrs. Bateman said Polly's response was that it did not agree with her husband to work in the shop and that he had concluded to farm for a while. She said it would be harder for him, and did not believe he would live a year. She told Calista that Henry had been hurt by a cultivator, which struck against a stone, and hit him in the pit of his stomach. Polly told her that Henry had vomited blood and had not been well since.

In the 1800s a cultivator was pulled by some beast of burden between the rows of corn. A blade dug between the rows to loosen the soil for the same purpose a gardener hoes his garden. The farmer would walk behind it, holding the handles on each side, while steering and pushing as the animal moved forward. Henry hit a rock, which jerked the cultivator, hitting him in the chest and stomach. According to Schubel, Henry told him he lay on the ground 3/4 of an hour before he was able to get up.

According to Albert, he was with his father the day he cultivated the corn, and rode the horse all day. Yet Albert said he knew nothing about his father lying on the ground. How serious was Henry's injury? It is hard to say. Eli Bickford testified that Henry himself had told him of the accident, but said nothing about lying on the ground unable to get up. Eli had no reason to lie about it. If Henry really had lain on the ground for 3/4 of an hour, Albert surely would have noticed it. Schubel might have added that part to make the cultivator incident sound more damaging than it was since Polly had used it as one of her reasons for Henry's illness.

Another supposed accident was that Henry hurt himself lifting some rails. This was part of Schubel's testimony, and part of the testimony of Abigail Filkins told to her by Polly, not Henry. We only have Polly and Schubel's word for this injury. Henry himself had told no one of this accident.

Julia's account of the arsenic incident, be it truth or cover, is as follows. "I heard a conversation between Hoag and Polly. Henry asked her to go to Dr. Bateman's and get some arsenic. Polly told him she did not like to have it in the house on account of the children. Henry said to her, 'You must be a damned fool, I suppose you had rather let the mice and rats destroy everything, rather than kill them.' I told her if she didn't get it Henry would be angry and the carpet would be destroyed. He also asked her if she would get some laudanum. She was gone two hours I think. I was there when she returned. She took the arsenic from her handkerchief and gave it to him and told him to take care of it. It was in a paper marked 'Arsenic Poison'. The laudanum she brought in a small 1/2 ounce vial."

According to Julia, Henry asked Polly for some meal. "He went upstairs, asked me for the meal and some water, which I gave him. He mixed the most of the arsenic with the meal and water in a basin. He put it between the lathing and the clapboards upstairs. Polly went out into the garden at this time I think. He put the rest on top of the clothes cupboard at the west end of the house," stated Julia.

We have only Julia's word for this incident taking place. Notice too, that she conveniently places Polly out in the garden while Henry was supposedly doing this, thus implying that Polly could not have seen where Henry put the remaining arsenic.

The laudanum, if really requested, was most likely for pain. Henry was starting to feel poorly again, and he was being treated by Dr. Townsend for cholera morbus. Polly blamed Henry's poor health on the farming injury.

Rhubarb, taken back then to purge the system, was also used along with laudanum as a treatment for cholera morbus. Be it laudanum or rhubarb purchased to treat Henry, it is not as relevant as the arsenic. Julia, in defense of her sister by the time the trials came, may have thought it best to say it was Henry's decision to purchase the arsenic.

Polly, on the other hand, at the time of the purchases, was justifying her reason to Calista for buying it. Polly told Mrs. Bateman she had some arsenic before but had lost or misplaced it.

Polly said Henry didn't want it in the house. Julia said it was Polly who did not want it in the house for fear of accident. Arsenic would not be an item you would carelessly handle, why say she lost it? Was that said on purpose in order to claim any poisoning from the arsenic she could not find as an accident? It is more likely that she told Mrs. Bateman she had misplaced it because she had already used what she had purchased from Dr. Bateman.

When Polly left the Batemans, the arsenic was in a small vial. When Polly got back home, Julia said the arsenic was wrapped in a paper. Albert would testify as well to the arsenic being wrapped in paper.

So, where was the small vile with the rest of the arsenic? Is it possible that Polly dumped the 1/2-ounce vial of medicine and replaced it with the poison? Thinking he was taking his medicine, Henry might have been taking arsenic instead.

Henry was sick for ten days before he felt any better. Selah Vosburg said that he went to visit Henry only once for fear he had cholera morbus again and he knew it was catchy. Selah said he had known Henry for a long time and had never known him to be sickly, although he saw nothing odd in Polly's behavior to make him suspect her of any wrong doing.

Henry's Aunt Abigail Filkins had also gone to see him while he was sick. Mrs. Filkins had known Henry since he was sixteen. Henry had told her, she said, that Dr. Townsend thought it was bilious fever (another name for cholera morbus) but he (Henry) did not think that it was. Polly complained to Abigail of the neighbors not coming to see him and that she had to care for him all herself. Was Polly looking for sympathy? After all, if Henry really had a deadly contagious disease, why would she expect people to come and visit? Simple—because Polly knew Henry didn't have cholera.

One could surmise that if Polly wasn't trying to poison Henry, and he was truly sick, she would want help with all the other things she was responsible for. Besides, if a person were going to kill someone they wouldn't really want witnesses around—unless, the poisoning was done discretely, and having other people around would provide for a good alibi.

In the rest of the conversation between Polly and Abigail, Polly spoke of telling Henry that he could never live on a farm. Henry told his Aunt Abigail that most of his fever was inwardly and he could not see what made him so sick to his stomach. Arsenic would have that effect on the stomach. We must remember too that Henry had had an accident. What if he had internal injuries and no one knew it? Combined with arsenic, this would be quite painful.

James Gumaer, the Hoag's neighbor on the east side of the farm, also went to see Henry when he was ill. James was there, as well as a neighbor Andrew Davis, during one of Henry's treatments administered by Dr. Townsend. The doctor gave Henry some type of powder for pain. According to James, Henry had a spasm so the doctor bled him.

Bleeding was a common practice back then. It was believed that the sickness could be taken out of the body by way of the blood. We know now, of course, that this has no affect at all, aside from making the patient weaker due to loss of blood. Henry did manage to recover somewhat but was never a very healthy man afterwards.

This seems to be quite a number of visitors for Polly to complain that the neighbors were not stopping by. All had said they saw no lack of attention on Polly's part towards her husband. It is our opinion that Polly did poison her husband, but not enough to kill him yet. She wanted all to believe that she was a devoted wife. Polly also wanted everyone to believe that Henry was a sickly man and would always be so. When she finally killed him no one would suspect a thing.

3

HENRY

After Henry recovered from his "illness", he decided to give up the farm and go back to the shoe shop. He may have realized that the rigors of farm life were too strenuous on his health. Since Polly's lover Matthew was no longer in Alabama Center, Henry might have thought it would be safe to take her back there. It would also please his wife to return to their old house at the Center and be closer to friends and conveniences.

On the first of July, Henry approached James McComb, another farmer, over the possibility of him renting the farm in which the Hoags were living. James currently lived south of the Center in what is now known as Basom. James said he and Henry made a verbal contract by which James would take over the farm in the fall. Henry told him he was going back to Alabama Center in October. Henry spoke to Schubel and told him of the deal he made with McComb. According to Schubel, Henry asked if this arrangement was acceptable to him. Schubel consented. Both Schubel and James confirmed at the trial that Polly knew this.

In July of 1856, Polly and Henry attended the Fourth of July Ball at the Alabama Hotel at Alabama Center. All would seem from appearances that things were changing for the better. Polly was getting off the farm and back to the Center where she wanted to be. The only unseen problem was that Polly still wanted the one thing she could no longer have—Matthew Bardwell.

To complete the circle of the deal, on July 10, Henry went to the shoe shop to see Eli Bickford. Henry told Eli, who was renting the shoe shop that he planned to come back to the Center in the fall and take back over his business. Eli then inquired as to Henry's health. Henry discussed the cultivator accident with Eli and told him that he was feeling much better now.

Henry was well on that Thursday afternoon of July 10, but by the evening, he would mysteriously become violently ill. Julia, who was at her father Schubel's house, went over to the Hoag home immediately upon hearing the news.

The following day, Schubel and Henry's neighbor James Espy, who lived to the west of the farm, went over to see how Henry was feeling. Henry told Schubel that he had taken sick the evening before and had vomited blood all night. James could tell by looking at Henry that he was very ill. To try and ease his discomfort James said Polly gave Henry some sage tea. Schubel, along with Julia, stayed all night at the Hoag's. The doctor, as of yet, had not been called.

The next morning, Saturday the 12th, Polly asked Schubel to go for the doctor. Doctor Townsend, the family physician, arrived about noon and Eli Bickford a short time later. Henry had a spasm while Dr. Townsend was there, and he prescribed some medicine in a powder form of which type is unknown.

Eli stayed to help watch over Henry whose spasms continued. Henry told him he had a death like feeling in his stomach and feared he would never get well. Polly prepared some broth and gruel for Henry. She told Eli that Henry's vomiting blood was caused by the injury from the cultivator and that Henry would shake all over, that he could not turn on his side without a spasm but only laid on his back and complained of being tired. Henry's spasms continued into the evening, according to Eli, and Polly continued to give Henry broth and medicine. Julia, Schubel, Schubel's wife Eliza, and Eli stayed until morning to help Polly with the care of Henry.

During the night, Eli Bickford was sent a mile and a half down the road to get Dr. Townsend but he was unable to come. Eli went all the way back to the farmhouse to ask Polly if he should fetch Dr. Bateman. Polly asked Henry and he said yes, so away Eli went again back to Alabama Center to get Dr. Bateman.

Figure 4. Alabama Center looking south, pre 1900.

Photo courtesy of the Alabama Historical Society, Alabama Museum.

This seems like a terrible waste of time, but maybe Eli was uncertain what to do since Dr. Townsend was Henry's normal attending physician. The delay would only benefit Polly's plan. The dutiful wife stayed up with Henry until two or three in the morning when she retired. Eli said he saw no lack of attention towards Henry on Polly's part.

Samuel Bateman did not appear at the Hoag farm until one o'clock the following afternoon. When Bateman arrived, Eli Bickford was still there along with Julia, Polly, and the Hoag children. Henry was in the middle of having a spasm as the doctor entered the house.

Dr. Bateman said, "Henry was lying perfectly still, and then he would jerk and throw his head back, he did not say much. He called for his wife perhaps. I gave him, I think, Dover's Powders and camphor, vermie valerian steeped; his pulse was nearly natural. He was not cold; there was no retching or vomiting. He told me he had vomited blood before."

Here we have to question the medicines that were dispensed. Dover's Powders contained opium for pain and ipecac, which induced vomiting. Why would the doctor give Henry something that would make him vomit all the more? He did not see Henry vomit but Henry did tell him that he had. The doctor most likely thought the proper thing to do was to purge Henry's system. If Henry did have cholera this would have been a disastrous thing to do. Based on their limited medical understanding of the disease, this is the way cholera was treated. Luckily for Henry, it helped get some of the poison out of his body. This would only serve to prolong his life a little longer, as Polly would continue to lace his tea and brandy with arsenic.

Camphor was a commonly used drug during this time. It was a stimulant. The vermie valerian had sedative qualities to prevent spasms. This to us would seem a strange combination to treat an illness; giving stimulants and sedatives at the same time.

Dr. Bateman knew Henry had accidentally injured himself in the stomach with a cultivator. At the trial Bateman would say, "When I went to see Hoag he had a very severe spasm; supposed he was suffering from an injury he received. I did not suspect poison. I would not have given the medicines I did, had I suspected poison by arsenic."

Possibly Bateman was implying he thought Henry had internal injuries which were making him ill, but there is no indication that he voiced an opinion to that affect. The fact that he would not have given these medicines if he had suspected poisoning leads us to believe that, combined with the arsenic, the doctors' care might have contributed to Henry's death.

Dr. Bateman stayed at the Hoag's for an hour and a half, and during that time he said he saw no lack of attention on Polly's behalf towards Henry.

Polly was obviously on her best behavior. She put on a good show to keep all suspicions away from herself. It was clever of her to look like the attentive wife; all the while she was drawing her husband nearer to death.

Julia stayed again on Sunday to help Polly tend to Henry as well as the other duties of the household. Schubel came by to see if Henry was feeling any better, but he wasn't. His condition worsened as the hours passed into the night.

Monday morning came and Henry must have known he was going to die. His spasms continued and none of the medication seemed to relieve the pain. Neither of the doctors from Alabama Center were sent for. Henry's symptoms became more intense as evening approached.

Supposedly Julia was present during a conversation between Henry and Polly concerning what he wanted her to do after his death. Julia claimed, "Henry called Polly up to bed and told her to get Matthew Bardwell and have him attend the shop and make up the leather; he said it would be the only way she could get a living. Polly objected, as people would talk. If Matthew did not like to board at the house he could board at the tavern. He did not think he would get well; while he still had his sense he would tell her what she ought to do. He told her to sell her crops to pay the rent with."

The fact that Henry would come up with the idea to have Bardwell in the shop, after all that had happened, is ludicrous. To think that Polly would care if people would talk, based on what she had already said and done, is equally unbelievable. This plan was not of Henry's making. It was contrived by Polly and backed up by Julia in defense of her sister.

Andrew Davis was also at the Hoag house that evening and sat up with Henry. Andrew himself did not hear such a discussion about having Matthew return to the shop. Of all the friends and neighbors who stayed at the Hoag's during the six days of Henry's illness, this grand idea was not told by Henry to any of them. Polly, however, repeated this as Henry's wishes to several people after his death.

Andrew sat up with Henry that night along with Polly and Julia. Andrew stated, "Henry had called for an herb drink; he told his wife in the night that he feared a spasm was coming on, she went into the room and rubbed him for about five minutes and he felt better for it." Andrew left the following morning after breakfast.

On Tuesday morning, the 15th of July, Henry did not feel any better. Despite the medications, which all thought would improve his condition; he seemed to be getting worse. That afternoon, Selah Vosburg and Mr. Bugby paid a call on Henry because they were concerned about his health. Polly was the only one home caring for her husband at the time of their visit.

Selah recalled, "She told us about his vomiting, thirst and pain in his head. We saw Polly give him something to drink and put a wet cloth on his head. She said Henry was subject to spasms and called it Cholera Morbus. I saw nothing peculiar in Henry's appearance, except one of his ears, which seemed black, as if blood had settled there. Don't recollect Henry himself saying he had Cholera Morbus."

Here is where the difference in symptoms of cholera and arsenic poisoning first become evident; the pain in his head and skin discoloration. Henry himself did not tell them he had cholera morbus because he knew that's not what he had. It seemed as such at the beginning, but as he worsened, he must have known cholera was not the cause of his illness. Remember, Henry had said he did not know what was making him feel so poorly.

This is the first instance, which we know of, where there were witnesses to the fact that Polly had been alone with Henry. Now was the perfect time to begin the completion of the final act. When Selah and Bugby arrived Polly was alone. She was just getting ready to give Henry his cup of sage tea, which she had just prepared before Selah and Bugby's arrival.

It was obvious to all that Henry was not recovering as expected. Schubel came by the Hoag's house later in the afternoon. Polly finally decided to call for Dr. Townsend and sent Schubel out after him. Polly had already administered arsenic in Henry's sage tea and knew that by this point there was nothing any doctor could do to save Henry now. For appearances sake it was necessary to request the doctor to come. Dr. Townsend decided that brandy was needed to drive out the illness and to numb Henry's discomfort. Polly gave Albert a bottle and sent him to Hescock's for the brandy. Albert said there was no brandy in the house before he went for it.

The doctor was gone by the time Albert got back from Hescock's. Albert handed the bottle of brandy to his mother, and then went outside to put the horse away. He was only gone a few minutes. When Albert came in he went into the kitchen and sat down and proceeded to eat the supper that Polly had prepared. Albert said his mother did all the cooking for the family.

Henry was lying down at the time, no longer having the energy to do anything else. The other children might have been outside or in another part of the house since Polly and Albert were the only ones in the kitchen.

According to Albert, his mother, carrying the bottle of brandy, walked over to the clock that was on a shelf in the kitchen. There was a small space between the clock and the wall where Polly removed a small folded piece of paper from out of her bandbox.

Polly opened the paper and poured part of the contents of the paper into the brandy and shook up the bottle. She then returned the paper to its hiding place behind the clock. Julia was wrong. Polly had known all along where the paper with the arsenic had been.

Albert asked his mother, "What are you putting into it?"

"Salaeratus," answered Polly.

"What did you put it in for?" asked Albert.

"To sweeten it," she answered.

Albert knew there was something not quite right about this. The salaeratus (now spelled saleratus), was kept in the buttery in an oyster can, not a piece of paper. Saleratus, which is basically baking soda and sometimes used to treat indigestion, is by no means sweet. Polly wrongly assumed that Albert wasn't paying attention to what she was doing.

Polly took the bottle into where her husband was lying down. Albert stated there was no one else in the room with them at the time. The young boy saw his mother lift the bottle to his father's mouth. Henry didn't say anything when Polly did this, just automatically took a drink from the bottle. Henry told Polly, after tasting it, that he did not want any more because it made him feel worse.

Albert, becoming curious, went back into the kitchen and removed the paper from behind the clock. He looked at the powder inside the paper. He thought it did not look like saleratus. Albert didn't mention the incident to anyone at the time. He might have thought it was some sort of medicine; and maybe his mother told him it was a sweetener so he wouldn't worry so much about his father.

As evening began to descend, so did the group of visitors. Selah Vosburg might have passed the word along as to Henry's condition to other friends and neighbors of the Hoags, as several people came by that evening to see Henry. Julia had arrived a short time earlier.

George Lester, husband of Polly's half sister Elizabeth, was the first to come by that night. He arrived just as the sun was setting. Polly requested him to stay all night. George consented and put his horse in the barn. Polly sent Albert to fetch Andrew Davis who got there shortly after dusk. All the small children were in bed by this time; only Albert, the oldest, was still awake.

Andrew's recollections of the event were as follows, "I sat up with Henry the night before he died. Polly steeped Henry some herb tea, at his request, to drink when his mouth got dry. He was feeble but got up once during the night. Henry told me he had spasms, and thought he was going to have one that night, but I did not see him have one. Henry felt sick to his stomach and tried to vomit but couldn't. Polly rubbed Henry and it seemed to ease him. I built a fire two or three times. I put a wet cloth on his head because Henry said he was hot."

George Lester concurred with Andrew Davis. George said that Henry seemed very sickly adding that Henry was delirious most of the time. Andrew's putting a cloth on Henry's head to cool him, while building a fire to keep him warm, shows Henry had a fever yet had the chills. George relayed that Henry complained of being very hot inside and cold out. Henry's tongue was dry and he was becoming delirious. All of these are signs of arsenic poisoning.

Remember that George arrived at sunset. He noticed one very important thing as soon as he entered the house; the bottle of brandy. George said, "I saw a number of vials and some tea cups on the shelf beside the brandy. I drank the brandy. Polly said it was good brandy. I don't know if there was any brandy in the house in any other bottle than the one from which I drank. I saw a difference in the color of the brandy in the tumbler and in the bottle. The brandy in the tumbler was a lighter color than that in the bottle. There were other bottles on the stand, one larger and the others smaller. Henry attempted to vomit an hour after I got there but could not."

Is it possible that the tumbler of tainted brandy being served to Henry was from the large bottle, and the other bottle from which George drank was fine? There was a noticeable difference in color between the two, which were supposedly the same brandy. It would make sense to have an extra bottle, one that no one knew Polly had, just in case one of the many visitors requested a drink. Albert had testified that he did not know what happened later to the particular bottle his mother had given him to get the brandy.

Schubel came back to the Hoag's at around 9 o'clock p.m. An hour later, George Lester rode into Alabama Center to get Dr. Townsend. Albert must have been doing something else at the time because he said he did not know who went for the doctor. Julia, by the time of the trial, will say something totally different in order to protect her sister.

Dr. Townsend administered calomel and brandy to Henry. Most likely he realized that Henry was beyond help and there was not much else he could do. He stayed for about a half an hour then returned to the Center.

Polly administered the brandy to Henry six or eight times during the night. Poor George unwittingly gave Henry the tainted drink as well. He served it a tablespoon at a time from the tumbler. George recalled, "Henry did not like to take the brandy because he said it hurt him so. Polly told him that the doctor said he must take it to drive out the cold."

According to Andrew Davis, Polly laid on the lounge all night next to her husband's bed and got up often to wait on him. She waited on him not to be a dutiful wife, as it appeared to all, but to make sure Henry continued to get his doses of arsenic laced brandy and tea.

At three or four in the morning, George offered to go again for the doctor if Polly wished him to do so. Polly said that if he thought a doctor would do any good she wanted one called. In the middle of the night, George Lester went once again to fetch Dr. Townsend for his ailing brother-in-law Henry. George immediately went back to the farm after speaking to the doctor. Townsend grabbed his medical bag—for all the good it would do him—and drove his buggy up to the Hoag's. Henry was at death's door when George got back. By the time Dr. Townsend got there it was too late. Henry was already dead.

4

THE MOURNING PERIOD

As soon as Henry died, Polly sent Albert to go fetch their neighbor, James Espy. James arrived at the Hoag's just after sunrise. Polly told James that Henry had been dead for a half an hour. Espy aided in laying out Henry's body for viewing.

Polly, dispensing with idle chitchat, was already thinking of how she could complete the task of getting what she wanted. James said, "Polly asked me if I knew of anyone to whom she could sell some cattle and cut her hay. She also said she would like to dispose of her home." Although these are practical things to consider, it is odd for someone to worry about it only hours after a loved one's death.

We can assume she was talking about disposing of the home in Alabama Center since the farmhouse belonged to her father. It was rumored that Polly and Matthew were planning to run away together, but this plan never developed. This was probably a fantasy on Polly's part since Matthew had long since ended the affair.

Upon hearing the news of Henry's death, friends and neighbors came over to the Hoag's to pay their respects. Julia, Andrew Davis, and George Lester were still there from the night before. Schubel of course had returned. Jacob Winslow, who was the town supervisor at the time, accompanied by Reuben Warren, came by a few hours after Henry's body was laid out.

Reuben testified that Polly told him, "She was anxious to see Matthew Bardwell and wanted him to carry on [the shoe shop]. She said she was sorry that Matthew did not come to see Henry before his death. Said Henry told her Bardwell should work up the leather."

Within only four hours after her husband's death, Polly's only thoughts were of Matthew. After catching his wife in bed twice with this man, it is doubtful Henry would have desired to see Matthew while drawing his last breaths of life. It would be equally hard to believe that Matthew would want to speak to the dying husband of his former mistress.

No one in town knew, however, that Henry had caught Polly and Matthew in bed together. This being the case, she already began to use the story she had devised about Henry requesting Matthew to be in the shop. Polly was obsessed with getting Matthew back.

Lovina Tabor, who lived at the Center, also came by that day to pay her respects. Did Polly act like the grieving widow? Not according to Lovina, who testified, "Polly showed me Matthew Bardwell's likeness, said he was a likely young man and that had been the making of him; she took it out of the trunk."

The likeness she was referring to was a daguerreotype, an early form of photography. What a callous thing for a woman to do. With her husband's body barely cold, Polly was admiring the likeness of another man in front of someone who had come only to pay her respects to a friend whom had just died.

The funeral was held the day after Henry's death. Robert Almay, the sexton, dug the grave which was thought to be Henry's eternal resting place, never to be disturbed again. This would prove to be untrue in months to come. The coffin was placed inside a box and a lid secured on top with screws. Henry was buried next to his children.

Figure 5. Tombstone of Henry Hoag. Alabama Center Cemetery.

Photo by C. Amrhein.

Because Henry had left no will, an administrator would have to be appointed and the estate appraised for its value to cover any debts. Two impartial parties had to be chosen as appraisers. Selah Vosburg, a real estate businessman, and Jacob Winslow were chosen for the task.

Selah went over to the Hoag house at the Center the day after Henry's death. Selah said, "We went upstairs and appraised the leather & etc.; she said she did not wish it sold, for she wanted Matthew Bardwell to make it up. That her husband requested she would have it done. Thought her manner towards her children was harsh on that occasion."

Obviously Polly's only thoughts were of how quickly she could get Matthew back. It would seem, by Selah's statement, the children were getting on her nerves and in her way.

Later that same day Polly went over to the shoe shop to speak to Eli Bickford. Eli testified that, "Polly requested me to give up the shoe shop by the middle of October. Polly told me Henry wanted Bardwell to work up the stock and Bards' could board at the tavern or the house with her. She told me Henry told her it would do no harm if she behaves herself."

Once again, Polly used the story she concocted about Henry's dying wishes. We know Henry would not have requested this because Henry already knew Polly could not behave herself.

The following day, only three days after her husband's death, Polly went to the post office at Alabama Center to mail a letter. She gave the letter to Reuben Warren the deputy postmaster. It was addressed to Matthew Bardwell at Wheatville. She asked Reuben not to mention it to anyone.

We have no idea what the letter contained, but we can guess. Within the past three days Polly had been hurrying to arrange everything in order to have Matthew back in the shop and with her. The letter probably contained the message that Henry was dead and that she had everything arranged for him to come back to her. It might have contained something else of more dire proportions that would not come into focus until much later. To the best of our knowledge, whatever the message contained, the letter was ignored. Matthew was already seeing someone else.

On July 26, 1856, Polly went to the Genesee County Court Building in Batavia and was granted by the court her request to be the administratrix of Henry's estate. Her father and Samuel Winchel, who was a friend of

Schubel Franklin and a shoemaker as well, witnessed the document.

It was ordered that Vosburg and Winslow would be the appraisers. With the matters of Henry's estate taken care of, all Polly had left to do was to solve the problem of the children.

The right of ownership of the Hoag house in Alabama Center would be divided equally among Albert, Rosalie, Frances, and Eliza Jane—not left to Polly. This was to help secure the youngsters' future.

Someone would have to claim guardianship of the children. This was customary back then since the man of the family was normally the property owner and sole financial provider for the family. Upon the father's death someone had to claim responsibility for each child under the age of fourteen. The guardians would handle the minor's affairs until they were of age to do so for themselves.

The mother was the natural person to do this unless she felt she would be unable to provide for them. If that was the case, there were a few options available.

One choice would be to find a family member willing to sign for guardianship, take them to their home, and care for the children and their affairs. The relative would guarantee the court that they would be responsible. If this was not possible there were two other much sadder choices.

The children could become indentured servants. This usually meant the siblings would be split up, and sent to whoever was willing to pay for them. This was a hard and often cruel life for a child, but a common practice in the 1800s. The last choice would be to send the children, and sometimes the mother also, to the county poor house.

In Polly's case there was still one more option left. If she received guardianship of the children, and they happened to die, Henry's estate would go to her. In her mind, the sooner she disposed of her offsprings, the quicker she would inherit it all and have Matthew Bardwell back in the shop and in her bed.

By Wednesday, July 30, Jacob Winslow and Selah Vosburg completed the appraisal of Henry's estate. The value came to approximately $1100.00, which included the property in Alabama Center.

Part of the appraisal listed the notes held by Henry against other people. There was also the value of certain possessions such as a gray mare, a one-horse buggy, a two-horse sled, tools and farm equipment, oxen and yoke, and one stove.

The crops Henry planted were a portion of the estate as well consisting of: two fields of oats, one on the east side of the farm and one on the west; a field of corn, and a field of buckwheat. Remember that within only a few hours after Henry's death, Polly had asked James Espy if he knew of anyone to whom she could dispose of her cattle, crops, and home. She was very anxious to keep her plan moving.

Certain property was set aside that was not included in the appraisal. The first groups of these were items of necessity for their everyday life. A spinning wheel and weaving loom, ten sheep and fleeces, yarn and cloth manufactured from the same, one cow, two swine and the pork of such swine.

They were allowed to keep certain household items such as cooking utensils and one stove kept for use by the family; beds, bedsteads, and bedding; one table, one sugar dish, one milk pot, and one tea pot; six each of the following: chairs, knives, forks, plates, cups and saucers; plus all necessary wearing apparel and clothing of the family, clothes for the widow, and ornaments.

Items of a personal nature, not to exceed $50, were also exempt. These included the family Bible, pictures and schoolbooks, and the family library.

The other group of property that was exempt, under the act of April 11, 1842, was anything of value wished to be kept, but not to exceed $150. What did Polly choose to keep? Was it anything of use or value to her and her children? No. Since she wanted Matthew back in the shop the answer is obvious. Polly chose to keep Henry's shoemaking supplies—one box of shoemaker's lasts (wooden shoe forms), one set of shoemaker's tools and bench, and a quantity of leather—total value, $92.

Polly's obsession to have Matthew continued as July turned into August. Her conversations with others were only of him, and the story was always the same.

James Gumaer had said, "Polly showed me a daguerreotype of Matthew Bardwell. Polly told me her husband requested, during his sickness, that Matthew should carry on the shoe shop, and that she supposed he [Henry] died before he was aware of it, or he would have told her more of his wishes."

Despite what Matthew was doing with his life, Polly was creating a future that included her ex-lover. Thinking that Matthew wouldn't like another man's children around, Polly began to lay the groundwork for their demise. Time was of the essence since Matthew was seeing another woman. Polly probably wanted everything in her life taken care of as quickly as possible before Matthew got too serious with this other girl.

In a conversation she had with Mrs. Barber, Polly reflected back on one of their earlier talks concerning the fortune tellers prophesy of the deaths in her family.

Mrs. Barber stated, "Polly asked me, 'What did I tell you! There has been one.' The child [Frances] was then sick."

Mrs. Barber was referring to the month of August after Henry's death. Polly's comment to Mrs. Barber, "There has been one," foretells that according to the fortuneteller, there was still another death to happen. Thus, the fate of one of her children is subtlety revealed.

We can even assume, since Frances was recently sick after the death of her father as Mrs. Barber states, she would be the first to suffer the same fate as Henry thereby fulfilling the fortuneteller's prophesy. The fortune given by Miss Orton that day in November would prove to be Polly's stroke of luck and the catalyst for her plans.

5

FRANCES

At eight o'clock on Sunday morning, August the 10th, Polly packed her children into her buggy and headed to Alabama Center to do some errands. On the way she stopped at Mrs. Bugby's house to drop off her two girls, Frances and Rosalie.

"The children stayed at my house until called for by their mother about two o'clock," Mrs. Bugby recalled. "Frances was a smart child. The children and mine played together. I gave them bread and butter, gave it to my children too. My children continued well. There was no fruit around the house."

The food the children ate while Polly was gone will soon become important. The fruit that Mrs. Bugby was referring to was green apples. If you remember, people thought that eating un-ripened fruit was a cause to contract Cholera Morbus with symptoms similar to arsenic poisoning.

Schubel was at the farm that morning when Polly left for the Center. There was a fire in the woods and Schubel and his brother-in-law, Henry Noble, were there trying to put it out. The fire, Schubel stated, was twenty to thirty rods from the house (330-495 feet).

Schubel concurred with Mrs. Bugby that Polly came back at two o'clock in the afternoon; however, he stated that the two girls came back at 11 a.m. not 2 p.m. with their mother. Mrs. Shepard, Bugby's daughter who was also at the house, agreed with her mother. She did not see the children leave the Bugby home while Polly was at Alabama Center. Henry Noble agreed saying he saw the girls near Bugby's and that Albert went to the Center with his mother.

Why would Schubel testify that the children were back earlier than Polly? Maybe he was trying to cast doubt as to the children's whereabouts between 11 a.m. and 2 p.m. If the children were unsupervised they could have gotten into anything by themselves.

At two o'clock in the afternoon, after Polly picked up Frances and Rosalie, they returned to the farm. While Albert turned out the horses Polly went into the kitchen to make the children some bread and butter.

Albert was not present while the food was being prepared. In Rosalie's own testimony she said, "After we got home mother gave us some bread and butter. Albert was not there when she gave it to us, he was outdoors."

Albert came into the kitchen where his two sisters were eating at the table. In reference to the bread and butter Albert said, "They were not small pieces. Frances ate hers all up. Rosalie ate part of hers and laid the rest on the table. Frances ate that afterwards. Mother did not give me any bread and butter; never did that I know of."

Rosalie had agreed with this saying, "She ate hers, I ate part of mine, Franky [Frances' nickname] took what I had left and ate it. We went out to play after eating the bread and butter."

A short time later, while the children were outside playing, the girls suddenly became ill and began vomiting. Seven-year-old Rosalie, who had only eaten part of her bread, was sick for only a short time. Frances, on the other hand, become violently ill.

While this was taking place, Schubel and Henry Noble were still outside attempting to get the fire under control. It was now getting close to dinnertime and the men were called up from the woods to eat. Noble went around the back of the house to the well to wash up.

Schubel, on the other hand, went around the house to the front door.

Schubel testified, "I looked and saw Frances coming from towards the barn; she ran up to her mother and said, 'Mother, I'm sick;' she took and sat her up in a chair. Pretty quick she began to vomit; I stepped along to the house. I looked and saw what she had vomited; it was quite a lot of green apples. Won't be positive if it was green cucumbers or not. I say to her, 'Now you see they have been eating green fruit; you can't dispute now but what they have been eating green apples.' When Frances first puked, Albert was out at the well; if I understood him he said she had puked a whole mess out at the barn."

According to Henry Noble, there were apple trees on the property and they were green but did Frances eat them? Even if so, it would not cause such extreme sickness. Schubel, at the time of the trial, testified that she did eat the fruit. Mrs. McComb, who came by the Hoag home later that day, said at the time of the incident she had asked Polly if Frances had eaten green fruit and Polly herself had said that she had not. Polly told Mrs. McComb that she had examined what Frances had vomited and nothing had indicated she had eaten green fruit.

Albert also disputed some of Schubel's testimony by stating, "Frances did not go to the barn after eating the bread and butter. Rosalie did not. I did not tell grandfather that they puked at the barn."

Once again, Schubel was trying to cast doubts as to the children's actions. He was the only one insisting that it was green fruit that made them ill, and placing them out by the barn out of sight, instead of in the direct care of their mother.

The girls came into the house, and feeling a little better, began to help their mother prepare dinner. While

Frances was paring the potatoes, she became ill and vomited again. The sick girl was laid down on the lounge while Albert, Rosalie, Schubel, Henry Noble and Polly sat down at the table for dinner. It is unknown where seven-month-old Eliza Jane was during all of this. During the meal Frances once again began to wretch. Polly immediately got up to attend to her sick child.

Polly sent for Mrs. Bugby to come over to the house to take a look at the children. Frances had been laid down on the lounge at this point. Schubel and Henry Noble had gone back out after dinner to the place they were having trouble containing the fire, thus leaving Polly alone with the children. Mrs. Bugby sent over her daughter, Mrs. Shepard, in her place.

A short time later, Schubel came back up to the house for some more water. He went inside to see Frances and talked to her for ten or fifteen minutes. He also said, "The little child seem to lay quiet."

Mrs. Reynolds, wife of the tavern keeper in West Alabama, arrived around sunset, riding along with Mr. and Mrs. McComb in their buggy. Polly went out to the gate to meet the two women who remained in the buggy, while Mr. McComb went up to the house to speak to Schubel.

Frances was still lying on the lounge, but no longer quietly. "Somebody told Adaline to be in a hurry, the little girl [Frances] then began to vomit," testified Schubel.

Adaline was sent to hurry to the gate to get Polly. Polly left the two women sitting in the buggy and came up to the house. She turned to Frances, and held up her head as the child continued to puke.

(We never were able to positively identify Adaline. By census records we did discover that when Rosalie was taken away she went to live with the family of Adaline & William Tyler. Our closest guess is that Adaline was a relation up visiting during that summer.)

Mr. McComb turned to look at the child as she finally stopped vomiting. McComb recalled in testimony, "Polly said the child had no physician. The child vomited while I was there; substance first green, then yellow, then that like slobber of a horse."

Schubel instructed Polly to get a mop and pail to clean up the mess, which she obediently did. With the incident under control, Schubel started out for the woods to return to the fire that was still smoldering. He went back out the front door of the house and down the path to the gate. Mrs. Reynolds and Mrs. McComb were still in the buggy as Schubel approached. As he passed them he said, "How do you do," and nothing more. The two women at this point must have decided it would be a good idea to go inside and see what was going on. Mrs. Reynolds stated, "I found Frances very sick, she was vomiting; matter was of a yellow-green."

It is here that Mrs. McComb questioned Polly as to the green apples, to which Polly said that nothing indicated Frances had eaten any. It was now dusk with only an hour of sunlight left. Since it was growing dark, Schubel and his brother-in-law Henry quit fighting the fire for the night. Considering the late hour, Henry Noble went along home. Mr. and Mrs. McComb left at this time also, but Mrs. Shepard decided to stay to help Polly with her sick daughter Frances.

In Schubel's account of what happened next, he testified, "Polly said Albert is going for the cows. 'Hadn't you better send for the doctor,' I said. 'I'll do just what you think is best about sending for the doctor,' she said. She said she had not any sage, I said I'll go to Norman's [Norton's] and get some. I got some and some turpentine at Mr. N's."

Turpentine in days of old was also used for medical purposes. They believed that if rubbed on the body, since it turned the skin red, that it somehow stimulated blood flow.

Although Schubel brought up the issue of calling the doctor, one was never called. Schubel stated he got the sage and the turpentine, most likely from Norton's Store in Alabama Center, but did not mention stopping for a physician.

Albert had been sent out to bring in the cows. He was then told to go to Alabama Center, to Schubel's house, to fetch Julia. Albert spent the night at his grandfather's and did not return until the next morning with his aunt.

Albert was not told to get a doctor, and Julia did not stop for one on their way to the farm. Why even send Albert at all? If Schubel went out to get the sage and turpentine, why didn't he get Julia and the doctor himself?

Figure 6. Warren & Norton Store. (Destroyed by Fire in 1921.)

Photo courtesy of the Alabama Historical Society, Alabama Museum.

Mrs. Shepard continued, "Was up nearly all night. Polly was also up. She gave Frances something she called sage tea. Rosalie had some of the same tea."

Polly was giving Frances sage tea, just as she had for her husband Henry. Most likely the same "blend" she had steeped for her husband causing his death.

Schubel Franklin agreed that Polly had given the child Frances the sage tea. Frances had vomited once or twice during the evening. Polly and Mrs. Shepard were up tending to the girl when Schubel went to bed. He got up once during the night to find both women still awake. Schubel went back to bed and did not get up again until a little after daylight.

Polly had plans for today—plans that at first, only Schubel knew about. Today was the day Polly had planned to go to Batavia to sign for guardianship of her four children. As the day's events unfold it will become evident that nothing was going to interfere with those plans.

We feel confident that Polly was poisoning her children with the arsenic in the bread and butter and also the tea. It would save Polly some time if the children would die right after the papers were signed. We feel she expected Frances to linger as long as Henry had. According to the indictments, Polly had given Frances almost the same amount of arsenic as she had given Henry. She was a small child however, not quite six-years-old. The effect of the poison would occur much quicker. Frances would die sooner than Polly expected, but it would not change her plans.

Maybe there was something suspicious about the way Polly prepared the bread and butter that made nine-year-old Albert choose not to eat it. There is no indication that Albert had any of the tea either. The baby was only seven-months-old and most likely not eating solid foods, and Polly might have thought Eliza Jane would notice something different if arsenic was put into her milk, and refuse to drink it.

It is our conclusion that the two girls, Frances and Rosalie were to be the first to go. Either Albert avoided what Polly made or maybe Polly needed Albert. After all, there were still the cows and the fields to tend to. As for the baby, her time would come when she began eating solid food. Unfortunately for Frances, who ate her bread as well as Rosalie's other half, she would be the first to die.

Polly and Mrs. Shepard were lying down when Schubel awoke. Polly told her father that she hadn't been asleep. Schubel said Frances' bed was in the same room as his and that he did not know where Rosalie had slept. If Schubel and Frances were sharing the same room it would be hard to imagine that he did not hear the women as they tended to the sick girl. We can only assume that Schubel had slept soundly that night due to exhaustion from fighting the fire all day in the woods.

Julia and Albert arrived at the Hoag farm at about six o'clock in the morning. Schubel saw them as they came in the house and they all sat down for breakfast. Frances was lying on the lounge as the family ate their morning meal.

Schubel said that his granddaughter appeared quite "smart and chirk" (alert and chipper). That Frances asked, or her mother asked her, to have some tea and toast. "Saw her take some from her mother," said Schubel, "said the tea smelt good and she wanted some."

Julia said nearly the same thing in her testimony. "Franky was laying on the lounge," began Julia. "At breakfast she [Frances] said, 'Ma the tea smells good, and I would like some.' Polly gave her the tea and toast. Said she felt better than yesterday."

Schubel already knew what Polly had planned for the day. He may not have known at that moment that his daughter Polly was poisoning his grandchildren. But when he took Polly to Batavia to witness her signature on the guardianship papers, he must have suspected something was amiss. As before, when the trials finally begin, Julia and Schubel covered for Polly in their testimony to make it appear that the child was feeling better by morning.

Mrs. Shepard, however, had a different account as to what happened the morning Frances died. Mrs. Shepard recalled, "In the morning the child did not seem any better. Frances cramped some, was thirsty, nothing was done for her but giving her the sage tea."

Schubel went outside to work in the garden after breakfast. Mrs. Shepard left a short time after that, about 8 a.m. Oddly enough immediately after Mrs. Shepard left, Frances took a turn for the worse. Julia and Polly were the only adults in the house. We have only Julia's testimony as to what happened next.

"Some two hours after breakfast she [Frances] appeared worse. Said, 'Ma I'm choked.' I gave the child some chamomile steeped in molasses before this choking. Polly got some salt and water and tried to get it down. I got some fetty, she swallowed some. Appeared to be a hard substance in her throat. Rubbed her with turpentine and camphor."

Let's look at the symptoms Frances displayed. Mrs. Shepard had said the girl was cramping in her stomach and thirsty. She had the feeling of a hard substance in her throat and of being choked. The vomiting, cramps, extreme thirst, and her throat swelling up with difficulty swallowing, are all signs of arsenic poisoning. The discolored skin, and her dry and coated tongue, would soon become visible as well.

Schubel continued with what happened next. "Rosalie came out and said her Ma wanted me," stated Schubel. "Franky was worse. Before I went in Polly came and said, 'Father why don't you come in! I'm afraid Franky is dying.' She seemed to be choked as if in a worm fit. Polly said she had tried to get down some salt and water, but she couldn't. She had got down a little fetty and rubbed her a good deal with turpentine. Polly did not think she would come to. When I first came in Polly spoke of sending for the Doctor; said she would have one at any rate. I told Albert to get the horse and go as fast as he could."

Julia corroborated Schubel's testimony by saying, "Polly sent Albert for the Doctor. I think she was dead before Albert and the Doctor got back."

"I worked on the child a half an hour," said Schubel. "I had to go to the woods to fight the fire; gone perhaps three quarters of an hour. When I got back the girl was dead."

Albert did not recollect whether anyone was there when Frances died; that he was there, and did not go for the doctor.

No matter who went for the doctor or who told him to come, the important point here is that Polly waited for this sickly child to breathe her last choking breath. She let her daughter suffer for hours on end before finally sending someone to Alabama Center to request medical help. The only quench for the girl's thirst was tea laced with arsenic and salt water.

What a sad death for a young child. Imagine this poor little girl looking up at Polly, her mouth parched, throat swollen, unable to speak; her eyes pleading for her mother's love and caring hand. Mommies were supposed to make it "all better." Frances gave her love to her mother, expecting the same, only to encounter a cold heart and the angel of death in return.

6

LIFE AFTER DEATH

Frances died on August 11, 1856. Based on the time frame indicated in the trial testimony, we can approximate Frances' time of death to be about 9:15 a.m. The child dying sooner than expected would only temporarily pose a problem in the timing of Polly's plans.

We know by records from Surrogate's Court that Polly and Schubel arrived at the court building in Batavia sometime in the afternoon. At that point, Polly entered her petition for guardianship of her children. Handwritten in the form was each child's name and age—even Frances'. The court set a time of 4:00 p.m. that same day for the hearing of the applications.

Based on the distance from the farm to Batavia by horse and buggy, Polly and Schubel had to leave the farm at least by noon. A lot would happen between 9:15 a.m. and the time they left that day. Polly was probably nervous and anxious to begin the trip to Batavia. With Frances now dead, prior to her trip to Batavia, she had to get rid of the doctor, the friends who came by, and still have Frances' body laid out before she left.

Mrs. Espy arrived at the Hoag farm just after Frances died, and testified that the doctor arrived shortly after her. Mrs. Abigail Filkins, Henry's aunt, came immediately upon hearing of Frances' death.

Mrs. Filkins recalled, "Polly told me the children were not well on Sunday, and that she had to go to Batavia on Monday [the day Frances died]. Supposedly they had been eating green apples, and that they [Rosalie and

Frances] were taken with Cholera Morbus after she returned."

Although Polly had originally told everyone that she was sure the children had not eaten green apples, Frances was now dead. She needed some reason for the child's death. Mrs. Filkins gave the first indication of knowledge of Polly's planned trip to Batavia that day. However, we believe Abigail did not know the reason for the journey. Granted, Polly had to seek guardianship for her other children, but if Abigail had known of Polly's intention to sign for guardianship of a dead child, as if she were still alive, surely questions would have been raised a lot sooner than they ultimately were.

Abigail continued with what transpired next. "I went in to see the corpse; Polly did not go in," stated Mrs. Filkins. She continued, "I removed the cloth from Frances face and put it in water. It looked purple. I told her it smelled like turpentine. Polly said they used it on the child. The neck and arms of Frances were spotted with purple. Her lips were dried and parched; think I saw blood on her teeth."

Abigail Filkins also recalled that, "Polly said that she had not sent for her husband's relatives in Chautauqua County because the doctor said it was not worth while, as it was nothing but a child."

We have no way of knowing if the doctor really said that, or if it was Polly's concoction. The name of the doctor who treated Frances was never mentioned nor required to testify. The reason for this was probably due to the fact that no physician was ever called to treat Frances; and when one was finally called, the child was already dead.

James Gumaer was called to lay out Frances' body that morning. He had noticed that the body was already quite rigid. Her skin was spotted and she appeared to have froth around her mouth. With this task of tending to her daughter's remains completed, and neighbors sent on their way, Polly set out with her father to Batavia.

Polly went before the Judge of Surrogate Court, in the same court building that still stands today, requesting her appointment as general guardian of her children. Just to clarify that Frances was knowingly added, a portion of the petition is below. The words in italics are the parts of the form that are hand written:

> TO THE SURROGATE COURT OF GENESEE COUNTY:
>
> The petition of *Mary Hoage* of the town of *Alabama* in the County of Genesee, respectfully sheweth, That *Henry Hoage* of the town of *Alabama* in the County of Genesee, died about the month of *July* 185*6*; that he left personal *& real* property, and *four* infant child*ren* who *are all* now under the age of fourteen years to wit:
>
> *Albert Burden Hoage aged 9 years the 15th of November last. Rosalie Imogene Hoage aged 7 years the 23rd day of July last. Frances Alma Hoage aged 5 years the 21st of September last & Eliza Jane Hoage aged 7 months*
>
> and that the said infants reside in the town of *Alabama* in the county of Genesee, and ha*ve* no general guardian. Your petitioner being the *mother* of the said infants is desirous that *she herself a resident* of the town of *Alabama* in the County of Genesee, may be appointed guardian to the said infants to the end that *their* estate may be managed to the best advantage. That the

personal property *of each* of the said infant does not exceed the sum of *fifty* dollars, and the annual value of the real estate of each of the said infants does not exceed the sum of *ten* dollars.

The petitioner further [illegible] that Shubuel Franklin of Alabama is the grandfather # [# continues along the margin] #*of the said infants and their only near male relative residing in the county & that the personal estate of said infants consists only of their distributive share of the personal estate of their father & a small house & lot of the value of about $500.*

Your petitioner therefore prays that she may be appointed guardian of the said infants as aforesaid.

Dated *August 11* 1856 *Mary Hoage*

The petition is consented to by the signature of Schubel Franklin on the bottom. We find his signature on the forms rather enlightening. Schubel was there in court with Polly, witnessed the petition, put up the bond for the children's care—all the while knowing his granddaughter Frances was dead.

To take time to consider Polly's request, the Court ordered that at 4:00 p.m. the same day, she was to return with her father for the hearing of her application. If any questions were to be asked or corrections made to the petition, the hours that passed while in wait for the hearing would have been the time to do it—but it didn't happen. The following is taken directly from Surrogate Court records.

In the matter of the Guardianship
of Albert Burden Hoage, }
Rosalie Imogene Hoage, }
Frances Alma Hoage } August 11, 1856
and Eliza Jane Hoage }
of Alabama minors under
the age of 14 years

On reading the petition of Mary Hoage the mother of said minors praying her appointment as the general guardian of the said minors. It is ordered that this day at 4 o'clock P.M. be assigned for the hearing of the application and that notice thereof be given to Shubel Franklin of Alabama the grandfather of said minors and there upon afterwards at the hour appointed the said Shubel Franklin comes into Court and consents that the said Mary be appointed guardian of the said minors respectively and the said Mary now in Court together with the said Shubel Franklin as her surety having executed a Bond to each of the said minors in the penalty of $200 conditioned pursuant to the Stature in such case made and provided which Bonds are duly acknowledged approved and filed. It is ordered that the said Mary Hoage be and she hereby is appointed the general guardian of each of said minors respectively until they shall respectively arrive at the age of 14 years and until another guardian shall be appointed and that letters of Guardianship in respect to each of said minors issue to her accordingly.

(*signed*) Joshua L. Brown

The guardianship papers for Polly's children can still be found in file drawer G1 in Genesee County Surrogate Court. There is a separate bond for each child, including Frances, signed by both Polly and Schubel. Schubel posted a $200 bond for each child for their care until they reached the age of 14 years and until another guardian shall be appointed. Normally, the text on guardianship papers reads "or until", not "and until", another guardian was appointed. Does this mean that all along Polly did not intend to keep her remaining children or was this a decision of the judge, concerned that Polly might not be able to provide for their proper care?

It should be stressed that even though Frances was dead, there is no indication that it was ever mentioned. Nothing is different in the guardianship papers of Frances compared to the other children. There is no mention of her death in the petition documents to the court either. As far as the court knew, by Polly's paperwork, Frances was still alive. Although it is only conjecture on our part, we feel the detail of one child being dead, so soon after her husband, was purposely left out so as not to raise questions by the court over the circumstances of Frances' death. We see no other logical explanation as to why Polly's petitions to the court included a guardianship petition for her dead daughter—and her father went along with it.

On Monday the 12th, or the following day, Frances' body was laid in the ground near her father and other siblings. With two deaths so close together and so many children already dead, the town's people began to wonder—but wonder is all they did. People did not speak of such things. It would not be polite conversation to talk of the possibility of your neighbor murdering her husband and children. Life in Alabama seemed to go on as it always had, except for Polly's.

Figure 7. Tombstones of the Hoag children. (left to right) Frances, Roselphe & Leonard, Viola. ***Photo by C. Amrhein.***

As summer turned to fall, Polly was to realize that Matthew wanted nothing more to do with her. On September 8th, Polly went to see Lucinda Farley, also from Alabama Center, to have a wedding dress made. Lucinda never knew Polly; she did not meet her until after Henry's death. Polly proceeded to strike up a conversation with Lucinda, a person she barely knew, spilling out her version of her tragic story.

Polly told Lucinda that Henry had been sun-struck and that is why he died. She told Lucinda she had lost a child to the same disease, and that they were both taken with vomiting blood. Polly next remarked to Lucinda that another child, although healthy, had only a short time and would not live long. It was a strange comment to make when speaking of a healthy child.

At the trial of Frances, Lucinda testified, "Polly had three offers of marriage, she said. She was to marry on

Saturday; [September 13] a saddler named Mayberry. That she could marry Matthew if she had wanted. I did not know who Matthew was. She said he was a man who had been in her husband's shop."

By all other accounts we know this was not true. Matthew wanted nothing further to do with Polly. If it was true that she could marry Matthew, why didn't she?

Lucinda continued, "The dress was to be sent by stage to Mayberry's address. But she then decided not to have it sent to his address but her own."

We only have theories as to the identity of Mr. Mayberry. We have never found any record in the town of Alabama census or town minutes for the name Mayberry, nor could we find him on the State census either. We have often thought that maybe Lucinda meant Maybach not Mayberry.

Polly's sister Julia married a saddler by the name of William Maybach in the summer of 1857, by Judge Duel in the town of Alabama. In the same place that Matthew Bardwell's (signed Bargewell) citizenship paper was found, was also a Henry Maybach. Henry ended up living in Oakfield, the town to the east of Alabama. When Henry signed his oath of allegiance he signed his name Henry Mayberry, despite the clerk writing in the name Maybach. Often there are spelling variations of surnames to be found in early records. It could be that Polly was to marry a relation of William's, possibly Henry Maybach, but she didn't. She didn't marry Matthew Bardwell either.

If not Maybach (Mayberry) or Bardwell, than who? Who was the third proposal that Polly spoke of? In September or October of 1856, Polly married a German man by the name of Otto Frisch. Oddly enough, William Maybach's mother's maiden name was Maria Barbara Frisch. The last name is too odd to be a coincidence. We had surmised that Polly married into one of the same families as her sister Julia.

Why was Polly in such a hurry to marry again? Henry had only been dead for two months. Usually there was a period of mourning. So why the big rush? The answer came in a newspaper clipping from the *Union Sun & Advertiser*, a Rochester newspaper, dated February 3, 1858.

The article relayed the death of Henry, Frances, Eliza Jane, and the possible poisoning of the earlier children. It also said, "Last spring an infant child - born subsequent to Mr. Hoag's death - died after a short illness."

Here is a very good motive for the murder of Henry. Polly admitted to her brother-in-law, George Lester, that she had not slept with her husband Henry in months nor would she again. Albert had caught Polly and Matthew in bed together on two separate occasions. Our only conclusion was that this was Matthew's child that was born after Henry died.

It makes sense if we look back on what had transpired over the last several months. When Polly discovered she was pregnant again she knew it was not Henry's child but Matthew's. After the move to the farm in April and before Henry's death, Albert and Polly had taken a buggy ride. She said she was going to the Center but instead went to Wheatville to have a private conversation with Matthew. She told Albert not to tell where they had been. It is possible that the pregnancy was the topic of their discussion.

She obviously received no response from that conversation. It may have started out that Polly had wanted Henry out of the way merely because she was in love with another man. Now having Henry out of the picture would be a matter of necessity. It would soon become obvious that she was pregnant again. How would she explain this to her husband? If, however, Henry was dead, there would be nothing to explain and everyone would think it had been Henry's child.

It would be interesting to see what the letter contained that she sent to Matthew from Alabama Center a few days after Henry's death—the letter Polly told Reuben Warren not to mention to anyone. Knowing Polly was pregnant, and with Henry now dead, it would make sense for Matthew not to have any more to do with her. Matthew most likely put the pieces together and decided it would be wise for him to avoid the trouble that was bound to be coming. The death of Frances would no doubt have confirmed his fears.

7

THE LAST OF THE CHILDREN

It was now a reality that Polly would have to resign herself to life without Matthew Bardwell. Her ex-lover was making plans to marry a local girl named Miriam Rogers, also from the town of Alabama.

The newly widowed Polly Hoag married in the fall of 1856, to Otto Frisch. Albert was now eleven; Rosalie, age seven; and Eliza Jane, just over a year old. The child Polly was pregnant with would have been born about January or February of 1857. According to the article in the *Union Sun & Advertiser* the child died in the spring.

Matthew Bardwell married that same spring to Miriam Rogers. They were wed in the town of Alabama on March 13, 1857. It is an interesting coincidence in dates. Did Matthew feel free to marry Miriam because the child Polly bore, which was supposedly his, was now dead? Or, did Polly do away with this child, the same as Frances, because Matthew married another woman?

The death of this unknown child might be the reason that Rosalie and Albert would be removed from Polly's care. It is unclear whether this was Polly's choice or if Henry's family made the decision to take the children from her. Whatever the circumstances, it was decided that Rosalie and Albert would leave Alabama. Tragically, they would be sent to live with different uncles. Eliza Jane was to stay in Alabama Center. Before summer turned to fall, the children would be separated forever.

There were many things to consider in the early 1800s before taking responsibility for another person's child. Rosalie and Albert were both old enough to help with chores, farm work, and any smaller children that a perspective family may already have. It would not be practical to take a one-year-old child. She would be considered an added burden to the already tough rigors of farm life. Therefore, Eliza Jane would stay with her mother and Otto in Alabama Center to await her fate.

The year of 1857 would be filled with change and tragedy for the Franklins and Hoags. The ties that bound them would be torn apart both emotionally and physically. The weather that summer, raining half the time with sporadic electric storms, would reflect the turmoil that these families were about to experience.

It was rumored throughout the town that Matthew and his new bride left the country and headed for Canada, but this wasn't true. Although people may not have known his immediate whereabouts, there is evidence that he remained somewhere in Genesee County for at least one year. Matthew Bardwell had taken his Oath of Citizenship in Genesee County on July 4, 1857. The couple left Alabama for Wisconsin shortly afterwards. Polly Frisch would never see Matthew Bardwell again.

This must have been a devastating event for Polly. The illusion she had been living under for so many months was totally shattered. There was no chance now for her to even contact him. Matthew had moved to another state, and Polly was tied to Genesee County by Otto and her children. We believe this event is what sparked Polly's desire to eliminate the remaining obstacles in her life that prevented her freedom.

During that same summer, at the age of 16, Julia Franklin married a harness maker from Alabama Center named William Maybach. William came to America in 1847 at the age of 14, with his widowed mother and two-year-old cousin, John Fidinger. They settled first in the Boston Hills area of New York State. They later removed to the town of Alabama where William learned the trade of harness making. Soon after their marriage, the Maybachs moved to Lancaster in Erie County, NY. Julia was not as accessible now for Polly to call on when she needed help with the children.

Before August ended, Henry's brother Lyman Hoag would come from Lenox in Macomb County, Michigan to take Albert away. It would be a cold parting between mother and son. Albert displayed no feelings whatsoever over the separation with Polly.

During the trial for the murder of Frances, Lyman had this to say, "[I] went to Alabama to get him; his mother gave him to me to do by as I would do by my own son. When I started with Albert, I shook hands with her; Albert did not; she told him to write to her as soon as he learned to write; [she] wished me to do so as well."

When Albert was questioned during the trial for the murder of his father, he was asked about that day he left Alabama and his feelings towards his mother.

Albert responded, "We parted friendly. I liked her well enough. Did not like her then, any better than I do now."

This is quite a confusing remark to come from a child. He does not suggest in any way that he cared for his mother. We feel that Albert knew very well what Polly was guilty of. There were no expressions of love, not even a handshake. It seemed a difficult task for Albert to imply that he even liked her at all.

Albert would leave that day for Michigan, accompanied by his Uncle Lyman Hoag without even a backward glance. Albert's grandparents, Warren and Hannah Hoag, lived there as well with Lyman. Aside for testifying at the trials, Albert never returned to New York State. He lived the remainder of his days in the state of Michigan.

Rosalie was sent to live with an uncle in the town of Ellington in Chautauqua County, New York. Henry's other brother, Warren Hoag Jr., lived there as well as several other Hoag relations. By the 1860 census she was living with the family of William and Adaline Tyler. We believe that this is the same Adaline that was at the farm in Alabama the day Frances died.

As for Eliza Jane, she was suddenly taken ill in October of 1857, as was Polly's new husband. With two children now out of her way, Polly was getting restless again. The odds of someone taking the now twenty-one-month-old Eliza Jane into their home was slim. Then there was Otto to consider, and he was now her husband. They were the only two things left standing in the way of her freedom. Polly was to return to the use of her favorite problem solver—arsenic.

The exact date of when Otto became sick is not known, but it was within a week of Eliza Jane's fatal illness. The following is taken from the *Genesee Democrat* newspaper:

> Saturday, November 14, 1857.
>
> ... after the death of her first husband she married a German by the name of Frisch, with whom she lived until about the middle of last month, when he was suddenly taken ill with the same symptoms of the others. He immediately sent for medical advice, who told him that he was poisoned, and upon applying the usual antidote for poison, he was speedily cured. As soon as he was able to get about, he immediately left the Country, charging his wife with attempting to poison him. ...

Otto did desert Polly that fall. What country he fled to is one of the mysteries that we were never able to solve. We assume it would either have been Canada or possibly back to Germany. There is no documentation to show if Otto had formally charged his wife or if he had accused his wife in general conversations with townsfolk. No matter, the fate of Eliza Jane would be enough to incite the people of the town of Alabama to act.

Poor Eliza Jane became terribly sick on October 4, 1857. Dr. Nelson Horning, one of the town's physicians, was called upon to attend to the small child. Dr. Horning came to see Eliza several times during the first week of her illness. He was becoming quite puzzled as to why her malady kept reoccurring. By his fourth visit, he found her with a severe case of diarrhea and vomiting.

The doctor administered calomel, and after almost two days she seemed to be better. The following Friday, on the 16th, he pronounced her nearly well. That same night Dr. Horning was called back to Polly's home. The child had unexplainably taken a turn for the worse. The doctor was stymied. He could find no physical reason for the child to be sick. Dr. Horning managed to relieve her distress, and again diagnosed her as being well.

The following day the doctor heard that Eliza Jane had once again taken ill. Within a few days Eliza Jane was as sick as she had been on his first visit. The small girl, not quite two, had diarrhea and was vomiting uncontrollably. The doctor did not know what to make of it. He saw no reason why Eliza Jane should be so violently ill. What the doctor didn't know was that Polly had been lacing the child's porridge with arsenic.

Eliza Jane Hoag died on October 20, 1857. This time the citizens of Alabama were not concerned about whether it was polite conversation to discuss the suspicious deaths of Polly's family. The town was in an uproar and everyone was talking. Could Polly really have murdered her daughter? What about Henry and Frances? There were too many deaths in such a short time for it to be a coincidence.

They may have closed their eyes before, but not this time. Eliza Jane was now dead too. They also began to wonder about Roselphe, Leonard and Viola, the Hoag's children that had died so many years ago. It was too late to do anything about their deaths—too much time had elapsed. It was not too late to do something about the death of Eliza Jane.

A year before the town had turned their heads, not willing to believe that a woman in their community could do something so horrible. This time they would not drag their feet. Once the questions were raised out loud immediate action was taken and events were about to unfold like spreading wildfire.

8

THE INQUESTS

Stanley E. Filkins, Henry Hoag's cousin, still lived in Alabama in 1857. He had recently passed his bar exam the same year Eliza Jane was murdered. Stanley was a 21-year-old aspiring attorney working with the law firm of Brown & Glowacki in Batavia. After the death of Eliza Jane, he wasted no time in contacting the Genesee County District Attorney's Office. District Attorney George Bowen, upon hearing Filkins' complaint, took immediate action.

George himself was a young man, only 26-years-old. He was born in the town of Shelby in Orleans County, which borders Alabama on its north side. After attending school locally, and teaching for two years, he came to Batavia to study law with the firm of Martindale & Bryan. George Bowen passed his bar exam in 1852. By 1855 he had joined forces with N.A. Woodward and formed the law firm of Woodward & Bowen. Aside from his own legal cases, he was now the district attorney for the county of Genesee.

In a time when everyone within miles was your neighbor, it is likely that George and Stanley already knew each other. Here was a case that, if prosecuted correctly, would surely advance both their careers. Polly Frisch, if found guilty, would be the first woman in Genesee County history to be hanged for murder. It would be necessary for the district attorney to move quickly and be as thorough as possible. The evidence collected in this case would be unusual for its place in time. Literally no stone would be left unturned.

THE INQUESTS

A coroner's inquest was scheduled for October 22, 1857 to investigate the suspicious circumstance that surrounded the death of Eliza Jane Hoag. Only two days after Eliza's death, Stanley Filkins, attorney; Robert Baker, the county coroner; Nelson Horning, the physician who attended Eliza during her illness; and seven jurors gathered at the home of Schubel Franklin in Alabama Center. The body of Eliza Jane was still laid out in the parlor.

Figure 8. Franklin home. Alabama Center.

(Extensively remodeled since construction.) ***Photo by C. Amrhein.***

The small town of Alabama buzzed with excitement. Now everyone had something to say about the suspected murders. People were putting the pieces together, and this time they had no intention of remaining silent about what they knew. The Batemans must have mentioned the purchase of the arsenic because it was immediately the suspected means of the death of Eliza Jane, as well as the other deaths in the Hoag family.

By court documents, and how quickly things progressed, it was obvious that they intended to pursue the suspected murders committed by Polly Frisch. Since Eliza Jane's death was the most recent, and she was not yet buried, this crime would be investigated first.

Through our research we found several court documents concerning the investigations into the demise of the Hoags. Although we do not have all the records, enough were found to be able to get a feel for what happened. The following is an actual court document taken in the inquest of Eliza Jane.

TESTIMONY ON INQUEST OF ELIZA JANE HOAG

> At an inquisition taken upon the body of Eliza Jane Hoag of Alabama county of Genesee at the house of Shubel Franklin of the same place and before Robert Baker coroner the following facts were sworn to by the several undernamed witnesses as mentioned below.
>
> Skiler Starkweather, sworn. Resides in Alabama. I have been in to see the sickness of Eliza Jane Franklin when the child was first taken sick. I came in two or three times. Since the child has been sick the last time, two or three times. The child kept making motions with its hands.
>
> Doctor Nelson Horning, sworn. I live in Alabama. I have attended upon this child during its sickness as physician previous to my being oathed upon. Saw the mother of

the child a few times Polly Frisch. She said that she was doing what she could for it. She called on me, was the 4th visit I found the child laboring under a severe diarrhea and vomiting. Also severe difficulty of breathing and coughed throwing up mucus from its lungs. Examined its abdomen and found tenderness other symptoms of inflammation of the bowels.

The first thirty-six hours I was not able to do anything for the child because the medicines were thrown up by vomiting. I finally resorted to the use of small doses of Calomel. Successful in arresting the vomiting by using Calomel. I gave it a large dose of Calomel to move the bowels. It did not cause them to operate. I resorted to injections.

The first - tossed off. The next three or four did not toss off. I finally succeeded in getting the bowels to move.

On the next Friday I pronounced the child nearly well. It was the same near night. I was called soon after and saw startings of the child. It was my opinion that there was no inflammation of the bowel. I could see no cause for that starting and twitching. I finally succeeded in calming the child. I pronounced the child well.

I again heard the child was worse in about 24 hours. I came in again about 3 or 4 days the child was vomiting again. I could perceive no cause why the vomiting and diarrhea should commence again. I could form no definite opinion what was the cause of its being taken sick again.

Testimony having been given by Starkweather and Horning, as well as others, the following decision was arrived at by the coroner's jury:

State of New York }
County of Genesee}

An inquisition intended and taken for the People of the State of New York at the house of Shubel Franklin in the town of Alabama in said county of Genesee on the 22nd day of October 1857. A.D. before me Robert Baker one of the Coroners in and for said county upon the view of the body of Eliza Jane Hoag and there lying dead upon the oaths of Stanley E. Filkins, Eli P. Vail, Alden Curtis, George H. Potter, Henry Preston, Aaron Barrett, & Alfred Losee; good and lawful men of the said county and being duly sworn to inquire on the part of the people of the State of New York into all the circumstances attending the death of the said Eliza J. Hoag and by where the same was produced and in what manner and when and where the said Eliza Jane Hoag came to her death do say upon the same oaths as aforesaid that Eliza Jane Hoag came to her death under suspicious circumstances and from some cause unknown to the jury.

On witness whereof, as well as the said coroner, as the jurors aforesaid have to this inquisition set their hands and seals on the day of the date of inquisition.

Alfred Losee, R. Baker coroner
Eli P. Vail, Stanley E. Filkins foreman
Henry Preston, Aaron Barrett
Alden Curtis, George Potter

Aside from being the foreman for the inquest, Stanley Filkins was busy with other duties. He had been requested by the district attorney to collect statements from the citizens in Alabama. Stanley spent two days gathering evidence in the death of Eliza Jane, three days collecting testimony in the death of Frances, and one week interviewing and recording statements and evidence surrounding the death of Henry Hoag.

According to Robert Baker's invoice, one week later on October 29th, he returned to the home of Schubel Franklin to hold an inquest in the deaths of Frances, Henry Hoag, and the infant child born after Henry's death. Something of a more gruesome nature would have to be done today as well. It was something that was not a common occurrence in the 1850s. The bodies of Henry, Frances, and Eliza Jane were going to be dug up.

Eliza must have been buried shortly after the inquest because it had been decided that her remains needed to be exhumed as well. Since she was the most recent of the deaths, the plan was to cut away a piece of her stomach for analysis to check for the suspected arsenic.

Although there is enough evidence in affidavits and bills submitted to the county to show that they exhumed the bodies of Henry, Frances, and Eliza Jane, only the casket of Eliza Jane was opened. There is no mention of going through with the exhumation of the body of the infant. The baby would have been only a few months old at the time of its death. It is feasible that they felt the size of the body would be too small to work with. Equally it might have been a decision of conscience. They might not have been able to bring themselves to go so far as to dig up a baby to conduct such a hideous deed.

Whatever reasoning was used to choose which corpse to dissect didn't matter. It was the act itself that intrigued the curious and caused a controversy. People were very mindful of their conduct in the eyes of God.

Religious beliefs and a close affiliation with any given church denomination played a large role in people's daily lives. To raise a body from its eternal resting-place must have been catastrophic to the religious community.

The overwhelming desire to know what was going on over in the town of Alabama, however, was greater than societies religious fears. The story received coverage in all the newspapers in Genesee County. Reporters from newspapers in Albany, Buffalo, and Rochester also covered the story. It would be interesting to know what Polly herself thought while all of this was taking place.

What Coroner Baker needed now was a physician with surgical know-how. Dr. Holton Ganson, born in Leroy, conducted a medical practice in Batavia. The Coroner's Office had relied upon him in the past for his medical experience and knowledge as a surgeon. Ganson was called to assist Coroner Baker in the procedure of exhuming the Hoag family.

On the 29th of October, after the inquisition at Schubel Franklin's home, Dr. Holton Ganson, Dr. Bateman, and Robert Baker, along with a coroner's jury, met at the Alabama Center Cemetery. The seven jurymen present at this exhumation were Wilson Smock, George K. Patterson, Stanley Filkins, E.P. Vail, Samuel Basom and J.E. Combs.

After the caskets were removed from the ground, Eliza Jane's was opened and the procedure began. Her remains were to be the first used as evidence of murder. An incision was made in Eliza's abdomen and part of what they believed to be her stomach was removed and placed in a small box. With this accomplished, the body of the two-year-old child was replaced in its casket and reburied. The coffins of her father and sister were replaced in their own graves without being opened. This would turn out to be an oversight on their part. There is no evidence to show that any type of autopsy was conducted on the other Hoags—at least not on this day. Once the tombstones were reset in their proper place the inquest was adjourned.

Ganson traveled back to his office in Batavia with the box containing the stomach of the young child. There he steeped the stomach in hot water inside a clear tin vessel and removed it to a pail. It was kept in Ganson's private office until it was delivered to Dr. Oliver P. Clark, a physician and pharmacist in Batavia. Clark was to perform a chemical analyzes on the contents of the stomach. Upon doing three separate chemical tests, Dr. Clark found what everyone had suspected. Arsenic.

In a matter of two weeks since Eliza Jane's death, enough evidence was gathered to present to the Genesee County District Attorney's Office. On November 9, 1857 Polly Frisch was arrested by Genesee County Sheriff Alvin Pease for the murders of Eliza Jane, Frances and her first husband, Henry Hoag. Pease, on behalf of the People of the State of New York, immediately set to work drawing a jury for the arraignment. Schubel Franklin, on behalf of Polly, hired the prestigious legal team of Wakeman & Bryan to defend his daughter.

The Batavia legal duo of Wakeman & Bryan were renowned for their reputation as an excellent defense team. William Bryan had formed a legal firm in 1851 with John H. Martindale; the same team of Martindale & Bryan that George Bowen had studied with in 1851. With the relocation of Martindale to Rochester, William Bryan teamed up with Seth Wakeman in 1852. The compatible strategies of the two men complimented each other well and were attributed to their lifelong friendship and success as a legal team.

William Bryan was the researcher of the two men and preferred to work behind the scenes. He extensively studied and prepared court papers, examined and scrutinized each case, and provided legal counsel.

Seth Wakeman, on the other hand, held abilities that shined in a courtroom. He was an excellent trial lawyer and a very convincing speaker. It was said that his strongest opponents in a courtroom found him "a foe-man worthy of their steel." Seth was always sympathetic towards the underdog and displayed compassion towards those who were placed in a situation of ill fortune. The case of Polly Frisch no doubt sparked the interest of Wakeman and Bryan from the onset.

As soon as Polly was arrested, Sheriff Alvin Pease began the preparation of the courtroom for the arraignment of the county's prisoners. Because of the sensationalism surrounding the case of the People vs. Frisch, extra men were sworn in as constables to keep the public in check. Eli P. Vail of Alabama was enlisted to serve twelve subpoenas on witnesses for the prosecution.

On Thursday, November 12th, Polly was brought before Justice Augustus Cowdin at the Genesee County Court House in Batavia. For six days Judge Cowdin listened to the evidence against Polly Frisch. Over the course of those days, ten more witnesses would be subpoenaed and brought to Batavia to testify. Stanley Filkins was present every day of the arraignment noting the testimony. District Attorney Bowen conducted the case for the People and the well-known firm of Wakeman & Bryan appeared on behalf of the defense.

The reporter for the *Republican Advocate* described Polly as "youthful and not unprepossessing in appearance, and asserts her innocence of this, or any like offences, and attributes the prosecution to local excitement and prejudice." The following is an article from the *Genesee Democrat:*

> She is 30 years of age, five feet high, small and delicate in stature, with black eyes, jewish nose, and a thin and

> compressed lip. She appeared in Court very modest and retiring, with her eyes cast down to one side, and her cheek slightly flushed, but exhibited no anxiety, fear or terror, and was apparently as calm in her feelings as a summer's morning. She does not appear to realize her awful position, and shows no symptoms of remorse or guilt; but seems to take the examination and proceedings as a trifling matter, and only seemed a little annoyed at the gaze of the multitude. She dresses in deep mourning, and was attended in Court by an old lady (probably her mother) and a brother.

Polly's son Albert was also in court that day. He had come from Michigan with his uncles, Lyman and Timothy Hoag. Albert only went to see his mother once. During the trial for the murder of his father he remarked about his visit with his mother in November of 1857.

"Saw her in jail; did not talk much, they allowed her to talk with me; she did not request me to come and see her; might have done so if I wanted."

It seems that Albert's feelings for his mother hadn't changed much since they parted that summer.

After days of testimony and reviewing the case that was presented to him, Justice Cowdin determined that there was sufficient evidence to hold Polly over for trial on the deaths of her family. Polly Frisch was removed from the courtroom and taken to the county jail on West Main Street a short distance from the courthouse. She would remain there until a further examination of the case was had.

Both the prosecution and the defense knew it could be the most interesting and important case of their careers. The team of Wakeman & Bryan would be formidable foes in the courtroom for District Attorney George Bowen. To convince a jury to hang a woman, and have that on their conscience as well as their immortal souls, would be hard task to accomplish.

For the defense team, it would be a challenge as well. George Bowen had studied law with William Bryan. Bowen already had an idea on how Bryan would handle the case and the methods Bryan used when preparing for a trial. The fact that the District Attorney agreed to have the bodies of the Hoags dug up showed Wakeman and Bryan that the prosecution had no limits as to what they would do in order to convict their client of murder.

9

THE EXHUMATIONS

In order for the prosecution to prove there was arsenic in the bodies of Henry and Frances, they would have to have their stomachs removed like Eliza Jane. Dr. Oliver P. Clark had already performed chemical analysis on a part of Eliza Jane's stomach. Dr. Holton Ganson, thinking the one test was all that was needed, had destroyed the other section. Since they were pursuing the prosecution of Polly on all three murders, Eliza Jane would need to be exhumed again for further testing.

Although Clark had previously tested for arsenic on Eliza Jane, he was only a local doctor. If Clark was used in court there was a risk that he would be accused of being biased and doubts could be raised as to how much he really knew about chemical analysis. The prosecution needed someone who was considered a leader in the field of toxicology. In order to convict Polly, they needed to put an expert witness on the stand, one with no personal connections in the county. Professor George Hadley of the Medical University in Buffalo would be the man for the job. His services would not be needed quite yet however; the bodies had to be exhumed first.

On November 28, 1857, several prominent men and a coroner's jury met once again in Alabama Center. They passed under the wrought iron arch beneath the sign that read "Alabama Cemetery", straight up the center aisle towards the back to the Hoag plot. Henry and his children were buried on the south side of the center aisle.

Figure 9. Alabama Center Cemetery.

Photo by C. Amrhein.

Some of the jurymen summoned that day were Samuel Winchell, Andrew Davis, Charles S. Shattock, Henry Preston, and Hiram Frary. Eli P. Vail also subpoenaed five witnesses to appear.

With so many caskets to raise and corpses to handle, more people would be required. Robert Almay, the sexton for the cemetery, was present. Along with him came Robert Baker, Dr. Holton Ganson, Dr. Nelson Horning, Dr. Samuel Bateman, and Reuben Warren.

Only a few of the men gathered here were physicians of one form or another and accustomed to the sight of a dead body. The rest of the group—be they assisting, witnesses, or part of the jury—were average men. It is hard to imagine what their thoughts were on the distasteful task that was about to take place. The last time the Hoags were seen they were living human beings. Now they were corpses rotting in the ground. Frances and Henry had been buried now for over a year. The stench from the decomposing flesh must have forced some heads to turn away in disgust, including those of the doctors'.

For whatever reason, the subject of the exhumation of the bodies was covered in varying degrees throughout the trials. During Henry Hoag's trial it was covered in vivid detail, but only mentioned briefly during the trials for the death of Frances. The trial for the death of Eliza Jane had been handled altogether differently than the rest. We can logically assume from Henry's trial that the procedure performed on each body had been similar.

Robert Almay, and most likely a group of gravediggers, began the task of unearthing the remains of Eliza Jane, Frances, and Henry Hoag. Once the boxes were sufficiently uncovered they were removed from the ground and set alongside their perspective plots. The coffins were enclosed inside wooden boxes. Almay had some difficulty getting the screws out because they had been rusted into place. The covers of the wooden shells were finally loosened and the tops of the caskets removed.

Robert Almay observed, "Think I could have recognized the body as that of Henry Hoag's anywhere."

Almay also recognized Frances as the same body he had buried and that it did not look like she had been disturbed in any way. Reuben Warren also felt that the body of the girl was well preserved and that he could recognize her as being Frances.

Dr. Horning and Dr. Bateman were there as observers and to offer any medical suggestions. Coroner Robert Baker had chosen Dr. Holton Ganson for the actual task of cutting open the corpses. The following is a description of the autopsy conducted upon Henry Hoag.

Ganson made no medical examination of the body other than to note that Henry was wearing only a shirt and nothing more. He immediately commenced with the incision into Henry's abdomen below the breastbone.

According to Dr. Bateman, "Dr. Ganson made two incisions six inches each; one lengthwise one crosswise; he put in his scalpel, and said he could not find the stomach; flesh seemed tough; it was not discolored but maintained its consistency. I did not make examination myself."

Dr. Horning, testified to almost the same and said, "Ganson...looked into it; did nothing more, that I recollect; he said it was all gone; I made no further examination myself."

When Dr. Ganson was asked why he did not proceed any further, he replied, "The reason why I made no examination was that the decomposition had gone too far. [I] have considerable expertise in surgery; arsenic would preserve animal matter, if taken sufficient to produce death would tend to preserve the stomach and prevent decay."

Dr. Ganson admitted, "Chemistry has not been a specialty with me. Two or three grains of arsenic would produce death; there is no difficulty in finding arsenic, when body has been buried a year."

Dr. Holton Ganson gave his medical opinion on the effects of arsenic on the human body, but he admits that it was not his specialty. Although he was a surgeon, he could not find the stomach either. In Reuben Warren's testimony he relayed that he felt that not too much effort was made to find it.

Based on Dr. Ganson's observation the matter was finished. Several people remained at the gravesite as the coffins were nailed shut and reburied. Robert Baker himself remained to see that the graves were covered and the tombstones were replaced at the heads of the graves. Baker held no inquest on the matter. Since it was already the end of November the weather would become a factor in the investigation. Coroner Baker decided to adjourn the jury until January.

Stanley Filkins was not present at the exhumation that was held on the 28th of November. It is evident that he was displeased with the outcome upon hearing about it. Nothing had been accomplished towards obtaining the most important proof against the murderess of his cousin Henry Hoag and the two children. Stanley wasn't satisfied and something was going to be done about it.

Filkins once again went to Batavia, this time to speak with the county coroner. He requested that Robert Baker make a further investigation on the bodies of the Hoags. The coroner called another inquest to be held at the Alabama Center Cemetery. This time a new jury was chosen. The date was set for December 14.

Despite the fact that it was only ten days before Christmas, fifteen jurors, four gravediggers, and three new witnesses met at the cemetery at the Center. Robert Almay, the cemetery sexton, was not present at the second exhumation; nor was Dr. Holton Ganson due to medical reasons of his own. Robert Baker was in attendance, along with Dr. Horning, Dr. Bateman, and a physician named Dr. Losee. Stanley Filkins was also at the scene that day. He no doubt wanted to be sure that the job of collecting the evidence would be completed this time.

It will be evident in the following description of events from Henry's trial, that none of the doctors had any idea which internal organ was which. They used Dr. Ganson's theory on arsenic preserving animal matter as their guide. The parts of the bodies that were removed and labeled as "stomach" would be their best guess.

The bodies of Eliza Jane, Frances, and Henry were exhumed from the ground once more. After the boxes were lifted out of their graves the covers were again taken off to reveal the caskets. The outer boxes of the coffins were so well fastened from the last time that the nails had to be pried out.

Next the coffin lids were lifted off and placed on the ground next to the caskets. This time however, the corpses were removed and placed on top of the lids. Doctors Horning and Bateman would conduct the autopsies on the Hoags. The incisions Dr. Ganson had made on the last exhumation were still visible. Dr. Bateman and Dr. Horning cut Henry open nearly the whole length of his body.

Nelson Horning stated at the trial for Henry how they commenced the autopsy. "We cut clear through the bowels twice. Had to use some force to open the barrel part of body; discovered part that was wholly by scalpel, it would not drop to pieces when taken out. It was my opinion at the time that it was a portion of the stomach. Some other portion of gall matter or intestines might have been mistaken for that."

Dr. Bateman describes the procedure, "We found what we concluded to be the membrane of the stomach: a piece 4 to 6 inches square of irregular shape, it seemed to tear from the spine, it was found at the place the stomach should be."

Dr. Horning recalled, "It was a decayed mass; could not distinctly trace anything, we secured something we pronounced to be a portion of the stomach; was found under the liver; took out everything except the liver."

Dr. Bateman continued, "The contents of the abdomen seemed settled down; the body was on its back the same as when in the coffin; did not exam as to heart or lungs; there was a small portion of the liver there; most of it was lying in a state of decomposition; the piece of the stomach was lying; a portion of it on each side of the spine, covered with decomposed matter. No part of it was discernible [sic] before the decomposed matter was removed. The freshness was directly under where this piece of stomach laid."

Bateman had admitted that he himself had no practical knowledge of the effects of arsenic on the human system, aside from what he had read in books. Based on Ganson's opinion that arsenic would preserve parts of the body, they removed decomposed flesh as well as parts that looked preserved. Bateman felt the other parts of the body they saw were the remains of the liver; Horning thought it was not the liver, but possibly the intestines or gallbladder. They really had no idea.

Dr. Horning explained the procedure further. "What we collected appeared to be shreds, partially decomposed. There was some hesitation between us, when taking out, as to whether it was part of the stomach or something else. Think I could not have told what piece it was if it had been brought to me, without knowledge of where it came from."

The contents of the bodies were scooped out with an iron spoon. Horning went on to say, "We secured all the contents of the abdomen we could. We did not scrape to the bottom."

A paper was laid in the bottom of a small wooden garden seed box with a partition to divide the box into sections. In one section of the box was placed what they had ascertained as the stomach of Henry Hoag. The stomachs of the two children were placed in the other section. The box was then labeled and given to Coroner Baker.

With this gruesome undertaking finally finished, the bodies of the Hoags were put back in their coffins and reburied once again. Henry Hoag and Eliza Jane could finally rest in peace, never to be disturbed again. Frances, unfortunately, was not to rest so easy.

10

HADLEY'S ANALYSIS

By that afternoon the inquest on the bodies was over. Robert Baker took the box with the grizzly remains and left the cemetery. Before he went back to Batavia, Baker stopped at the saddle shop at Alabama Center. There were several people there milling around the shop. The coroner no doubt wanted to let the citizens of Alabama know that the dreadful deed was finished. One has to wonder if there was some desire on Baker's part to share all the gory details as well. Such a bizarre event would certainly have stirred excitement and unlimited discussions on the pros and cons of exhuming corpses.

It was getting late when Robert Baker left Alabama for the trek back to Batavia. Due to the late hour at which he arrived home, he decided to wait until the next day to deliver the box to Oliver P. Clark. He placed the putrid smelling box in a cupboard in the back room of his home overnight. His family knew nothing of what he brought into their house. It was probably a wise idea not to let his wife know that he had such a horrid thing in their home.

The next day Robert delivered the seed box to O. P. Clark at his drugstore in Batavia. Clark was to deliver this along with Polly's bandbox to Professor George Hadley. A bandbox is what women kept their collars in, and in Polly's case, allegedly the arsenic. Because of the type of transportation available, the logical guess is that Clark caught the New York Central Railroad train in Batavia for the trip to Buffalo to deliver the boxes to Professor George Hadley. He most likely would have taken the stage from the train station to reach the medical college, now known as the State University of New York at Buffalo. On December 28, 1857 O.P. Clark arrived at the college located at Winspear and Kensington Avenues in Buffalo. He handed over the internal remains of the Hoags to Hadley for analysis.

George Hadley, born in 1813, was the University's first Professor of Chemistry and Pharmacy. He began his career studying with an engineer on the Erie Canal in 1841 and also worked on reports in the canal office in Albany. Hadley was very adept in the field of chemistry and mineralogy. He held a position for a short time as a professor of those fields at the University of Missouri.

Hadley honed his talents attending lectures on chemistry and geology in New Haven, Connecticut. He later spent time conducting research on various minerals while working for the Canadian Mining Company on Lake Superior. Professor George Hadley was appointed to the University at Buffalo in 1846 and held the position until his death in 1877. He is among the founding faculty of the school.

Prof. Hadley was admitted to the Erie County Medical Society in 1856. He already had a reputation as an expert in his field. He was the perfect choice for the prosecution to use to conduct the chemical analysis on the remains of the Hoags. The fact that his lectures were clear, scientific, and accurate earned him the reputation as an excellent witness in testimony as an expert in toxicology.

Aside from his lectures at the University of New York at Buffalo, he lectured at Middlebury College and Castletown Medical College, both in Vermont. Hadley's attendance at these universities in Vermont in the year of 1858 would turn out to be a catastrophe for District Attorney George Bowen.

The professor spent the month of January 1858 conducting chemical tests to detect any traces of arsenic in the pieces of the internal organs he was given. For those readers interested in such things we have included a portion of Professor George Hadley's testimony describing the said testing for arsenic.

"I mixed the remains in a glass bottle with alcohol; after standing a few days I took a part and concentrated it so as to reduce the bulk, and filtered to get a clear solution. To this I added a little muristic [sic] acid and boiled it with copper foil, then washed the foil clean and introduced it into a glass tube which I heated and the foil became bright, and a sublimate of arsenic condensed on the tube above. On examination of this sublimate with the microscope I thought I detected arsenical crystals; from this I suspected arsenic."

Hadley continued further, "A clear solution of the alcohol containing the remains was concentrated, to which I added a little sulfuric acid and put it in a little pure zinc in a bottle when hydrogen gas was evolved; this I caused to pass through a small glass tube leading from the bottle, a part of which was heated red hot; expecting that if the hydrogen contained arsenic it would be deposited in the glass tube beyond the heated portion, forming a ring having the characteristic metallic luster, which indicates this mineral - this I found to be the case."

Hadley concluded his description of his testing. "I afterwards ignited the jet of hydrogen as it passed from the tube, and bringing a cold plate of glass down upon the flame, a stain of arsenic became perceptible on the glass. The tubes containing the metallic ring obtained by passing the gas through while heated, I next sealed at both ends by melting the glass, and by gently heating them, the arsenic that formed the ring was oxidized and appeared in clear white crystals of arsenious acid, or white arsenic.—This is regarded as a conclusive test."

By the result of all these tests, Hadley came to the conclusion that arsenic was present in the bodies. The exact amount of arsenic was not ascertained at this time. Hadley's time frame was short in order to be ready for the Court of Sessions scheduled to be held on February first.

Based on the experiments, however, Hadley had a basic idea of the amount by the residue of arsenic that was visible after the analysis. In Henry's body there was a small amount, in Eliza Jane barely detectable, in Frances there was a very large quantity.

The prosecution intended to try their suspect on the murder of Henry first. This was the case in which the prosecution felt they had the most evidence and a large number of witnesses. Because of this, Hadley focused his attentions on the remains of Henry. At this point, he concluded enough from his chemical analysis for the District Attorney to seek murder indictments against Polly Frisch.

11

THE INDICTMENTS

Coroner Robert Baker was back in Alabama again. The Coroner's jury was reconvened on January 19, 1858. The inquest was held at the Alabama Hotel, now owned by David J. Duel. It would last for two days.

The hotel, the ballroom, and even his house were full to the brim with people. Aside from the jury, twenty witnesses had been called for the 19th and fourteen more the following day. Local excitement and activity encompassed Alabama Center. When Duel submitted his bill to the county, he expressed his annoyance with the amount of people that tracked through his place for those two days.

David Duel had commented on his bill, "They use my ballroom and the whole house besides & the charges I have made will not make me whole. The house was very much crowded, benches broken, & it was a muddy dirty time."

Muddy and wet but not snowy like they had expected for a January in this part of New York State. The unseasonably mild winter had made it possible to exhume the bodies in the middle of December. The weather continued well, cool but not cold, so the inquest was held earlier than would have normally been possible.

February was equally as pleasant as the previous months and an early spring was predicted. Polly Frisch, unfortunately, would not be able to enjoy it. The inquest was now completed with satisfactory results. Sheriff Pease had telegraphed Professor George Hadley to have him relay his findings. Hadley had completed enough testing to verify that there had indeed been arsenic present in the bodies.

Figure 10. Alabama Hotel, early 1900s. Built in the 1840s, the Alabama Hotel restaurant is still in operation under the same name. ***Photo courtesy of the Alabama Historical Society, Alabama Museum.***

On the first day of the month Polly was brought before the Court of Sessions at the County Court House in Batavia. The members of the Court of Sessions, which presided over the case, were Judge Joshua L. Brown and two Justices of the Peace, John G. Bixby and William Barrett.

The jurors in the case for the People vs. Polly Frisch on the indictments for murder were as follows: Amaziah Jenkins (Foreman), Sherrock Parker, Charles H. Monell, Rufus Carter, Thomas J. Stephenson, John Sprague, Charles A. Russell, Ami

Andrews, Horace Sumner, Seneca Allen, Jabin Bosworth, Warren C. Rowley, Russell Thorp, Miles G. White, Gideon Howland, Arza Newell, Thomas D. Waldo, Alexander H. Foster, John Sumner, James D. Benham, and E.W. Godey. Twenty-one men in all were empanelled for the jury and a total of thirty-four witnesses called to testify. The Grand Jury was in session for two days.

Polly was indicted on three separate charges of murder in the first degree for the murders of Henry, Frances, and Eliza Jane Hoag. The beginning of each indictment is similar, and the text in each as it progresses becomes very redundant, each one taking ten handwritten legal size pages. Only an excerpt from each will be given here.

> *INDICTMENT for the murder of Henry Hoag.*
>
> The jurors for the people of the State of New York and for the body of the county of Genesee to wit [*names given above*] then and there being duly sworn and charged upon their oath present that Polly Frisch late of the town of Alabama and the county of Genesee aforesaid- not having the fear of God before her eyes but being moved and seduced by the instigation of the devil and of her malice aforethought wickedly, contrivingly [sic] and intending one Henry Hoag with poison willfully feloniously and of her malice aforethought to kill and murder heretofore wit: on the eighth day of July one thousand eight hundred and fifty six with force and arms ... a large quantity

of a certain deadly poison called white arsenic to wit two drachms of the said white arsenic did put mix and mingle with a certain quantity of sage tea ... being one pint ... and that the said Polly Frisch ...did solicit ask persuade and instigate the said Henry Hoag to drink and swallow down the said sage tea... he the said Henry Hoag not knowing the said sage tea to be so poisoned did and there did drink take and swallow down ...and there became sick and greatly disturbed in his body ... and the said Henry Hoag ... did languish and languishing did live until the fifteenth day of July ...and of the sickness occasioned thereby died.

... the said Polly Frisch...with premeditated design to effect the death of the said Henry Hoag ... a large quantity of arsenic did put mix and mingle into and with a certain quantity of Brandy...and the said Henry Hoag swallowed down a large quantity to wit one half a pint... at the time he so took the brandy not knowing there was any arsenic or any other poisonous or hurtful ingredient mixed or mingled with the said brandy. That the said Henry Hoag then and there became mortally sick and distempered in his body ... and of the mortal sickness occasioned thereby on the said eighth day of July ...did languish and languishing did live until the 15th day of July ...thereby as aforesaid did die.

INDICTMENT for the murder of Frances Hoag.

The jurors [*mentioned above*] ... then and there being sworn and charged to inquire for the people of the said state and for the body of the county aforesaid upon their oath present that Polly Frisch ...not having the fear of God before her eyes but being moved and seduced by the instigation of the devil and of her malice aforethought wickedly contrived and intending one Frances Hoag with poison willfully feloniously and of her malice aforethought to kill and murder heretofore to wit: On the fifteenth day of August in the year of our Lord one thousand eight hundred and fifty-six with force and arms ... a large quantity of a certain deadly poison called white arsenic did put mix and mingle into and with a certain quantity of sage tea ... and that the said Polly Frisch ... did solicit ask and persuade and instigate the said Frances Hoag to drink and swallow down the said sage tea ... she the said Frances Hoag not knowing the said sage tea to be poisoned did then and there take drink, and swallow down ... by means whereof ... became sick and greatly distressed in her body ... and of the sickness occasioned thereby on the said fifteenth day of August ... did languish and languishing did live and on the sixteenth day of August ...of the said poison and of the sickness occasioned thereby died.

INDICTMENT for the murder of Eliza Jane Hoag.

The jurors ... then and there being duly sworn and charged upon their oath present that Polly Frisch ... not having the fear of God before her eyes but being moved and seduced by the instigation of the devil and of her malice aforethought wickedly contrivingly and intended on Eliza Jane Hoag with poison willfully feloniously and of her malice aforethought to kill and murder heretofore to wit: on the fourth day of October in the year one thousand eight hundred and fifty seven with force and arms ... a large quantity of a certain deadly poison called white arsenic to wit two drachms of the said white arsenic did put mix and mingle into and with a certain quantity of porridge .. and that the said Polly Frisch did solicit ask persuade and instigate the said Eliza Jane Hoag ... to swallow down the said porridge ... the said Eliza Jane not knowing the said porridge to be so poisoned ... did take and swallow down ... and of the sickness occasioned thereby on the said forth day of October ... did languish and languishing did live until the twentieth day of October ... on which said twentieth day of October ... the said Eliza Jane ... of the sickness occasioned thereby died.

It should be noted that the date of death for Frances and Henry was incorrectly stated in the indictments written by District Attorney Bowen. Trial testimony as well as cemetery records verify that Frances died on August eleventh, not the fifteenth; and that Henry died on the sixteenth not the fifteenth. In his haste to have the three indictments ready by the first of February, it is possible District Attorney Bowen had confused the dates.

This could be the reason no one caught on that Polly had applied for the guardianship of Frances after the child was already dead. Since the indictment states the 15th as her date of death, it would appear that the guardianship papers had been filed four days earlier to her death rather than on the day she died.

Each indictment also mentions that Polly had mixed the arsenic with another substance "to the jurors unknown." This was probably stated to cover any poison she may have added to the food that they were unaware of. The arsenic being mixed into the bread and butter would not be revealed until the actual trials commenced.

Within the indictments it is written that the jurors had rendered their verdict that Polly Frisch had indeed poisoned the members of her family with arsenic. Foreman, Amaziah Jenkins, signed the back of each indictment certifying that they were true and that the jury had concurred. It is also written on the three indictments, "The Prisoner on being arraigned demands a trial."

On February 3, 1858, Polly Frisch was brought back into court to hear the verdict. Polly was held over for trial on three counts of murder in the first degree. With the verdict so rendered, Polly was returned to jail to await her fate.

Before the indictments were even filed in the clerk's office, the news was out. A reporter from the

Genesee Democrat newspaper had leaked the story to Rochester's *Union Sun & Advertiser* about the goings on in Alabama. In comparison to official documents it is the closest account to what really happened.

The correspondent was in Alabama the day after the inquest on the 29th of January. The article in this weekly newspaper was printed in the Wednesday, February 3rd issue, a portion of which is given here.

> *Arrest of a Woman in Genesee County Charged with Poisoning Her Husband and Six Children*
>
> A correspondent of the *Democrat,* writing from Alabama, Genesee County, 30th, gives the following account of the investigation into a horrible poisoning case which has just come to light in that locality.—
>
> Some time in July 1857, Henry Hoag, a respectable citizen of this town, died quite suddenly.— About six weeks after his death a little daughter, five or six years old, died after an illness of only twenty-four hours. Suspicions of foul play were entertained by some at the time, but no action was taken in the case. Last spring an infant child—born subsequent to Mr. Hoag's death—died after a short illness. Suspicion was again aroused, but nothing done. Last fall another child; some two years old, died under still more suspicious circumstances. ...
>
> Some years since, three other of her children died, quite suddenly with

> symptoms almost precisely similar to the last ones, and it is inferred, that she poisoned them also, from the fact that she confessed that she had poisoned the first one, but that she did it accidentally and through mistake. All together this is one of the most horrid cases on record.

It is only conjecture of course as to whether Polly actually said that to anyone, as it never was mentioned in witness testimony. The Saturday, February 6th issue of the *Genesee Democrat* newspaper reported the following.

> The Grand Jury had a large quantity of business before them. Among the rest was the alleged murder in Alabama. We understand that they found an indictment against Polly Hoag, for the murder of her children. She will probably be tried at the Circuit Court, to be held here on the second Monday of March.

The article wasn't totally accurate, but all the facts were not yet known. They were not aware there was also an indictment on the murder of her husband. On February 9, 1858 the indictment papers were filed in the Genesee County Clerk's Office.

> Entered in the Ledger of Minutes of
> Sessions 1844-1858.
>
> February 9, 1858, 10:00 a.m.,
> 3 indictments,
> The People -Vs- Polly Frisch
> To be held March 26, 1858.

The March date refers to when the trial was slated to be held. The prosecution planned on trying Polly for the murder of her husband Henry Hoag first. It appeared to be their strongest case. At this point District Attorney Bowen thought he had enough evidence to convict Polly the first time out. He did not imagine that he would have to bring the other cases to trial. There was no way that Bowen could have known that this was only the beginning.

12

HENRY'S TRIAL - The Prosecution

Polly's outward appearance to the court during her arraignment was one of cool composure, but the reality of her situation was having its effect. Circuit Court was scheduled for March 26, 1858. Polly would not be in attendance that day. Whether real or imagined, Polly became ill. Dr. Oliver P. Clark, on the request of Sheriff Pease, was called in to examine Polly. For five days, from March 9th to March 13th, Dr. Clark tended to whatever aliment it was that troubled her.

Seven constables were sworn in on March 8th to assist with the various upcoming cases. They were Isaac Storms, A.B. Pease, Oliver Parrish, N.A. Sutton, Charles Sprague, Lorenzo Olcott, and Hamilton Driggs. Part of their duties were to bring the defendants to court, attend the trials, and travel to subpoena witnesses. Often the witnesses were picked up and brought into court. There were five witnesses that Sheriff Pease had already subpoenaed and one by Olcott, all for the Frisch case. As it would turn out the witnesses would have to wait to tell what they knew about the deaths in the Hoag family. Polly was still displaying symptoms from some illness the closer her court date came. Because of her ailment, Dr. Clark declared her to be too sick to stand trial. The defendant's court date was rescheduled for the June term.

The *Republican Advocate* of Genesee County reported in their March 16th issue, the following story:

> The March Term of the Court of Oyer and Terminer, commenced on Monday of last week, Judge Grover presiding.—A pretty large amount of business has been done, and considerable is yet on the calendar. The woman Friesch [sic], charged with the murder of her husband and children, is to be tried this week, if she recovers sufficiently from her illness. She has been quite sick for some days, and it is doubtful if she gets well very soon.
>
> Since the above was in type, we have learned that the trial of Mrs. Friesch [sic] has been put off until the June Term.

At that time the text for printing a newspaper page was manually type set by individual lead letters. The last paragraph of the article was placed at the end, rather than resetting the entire column.

Polly Frisch was reprieved once again. It was hoped that this would give the doctor enough time to treat Polly and make her fit enough to attend court. The postponement was a blessing for the prosecution. They would now have extra time to enlist more witnesses and prepare a stronger case.

Polly's physician had been changed from Dr. Oliver P. Clark to Dr. John Cotes. Dr. Clark had done the first chemical analysis for arsenic on one of the defendant's children for the prosecution. It might be perceived as a conflict of interest to have Dr.

Clark treat Polly for her illness. Too many assumptions would be made as to conversations they may have had or the type of medicine being prescribed. It was probably thought that the best thing would be to switch to a physician that had not been directly involved in the case.

Figure 11. Old Genesee County Jail. No longer standing. Originally on the corner of Main & Oak (now Route 98) streets in the city of Batavia, approximately where Oliver's Candies is now located.

Photo courtesy of the Genesee County History Department.

Dr. Cotes visited Polly Frisch several times during the next two months. He tended to her at the jail during the month of April from the 9th till the 15th, and again for four days towards the end of the month. On every visit it is stated in Dr. Cotes' bill to the county that he administered medicine. What type of medicine or what aliment it was supposed to treat is unknown. She seemed to be feeling better by the beginning of May. To be sure she would be ready for trial, Dr. Cotes examined Polly at the jail twice in May and once on the 6th of June. This time there would be no postponement.

Stanley Filkins was still assisting the District Attorney's Office with their case against Polly Frisch. Aside from the three days Stanley attended court, he spent an extra six days gathering more testimony. By the end of June, Sheriff Pease had served subpoenas on an additional forty-one witnesses. Albert Hoag was to be one of them and his testimony would prove to be the most startling.

Albert, who was now almost twelve, had arrived from Michigan accompanied by his Uncle Lyman Hoag. Sheriff Pease had gone to Michigan personally on the 27th to get him. It took three days to make the round trip, we imagine by train. Lyman hadn't told Albert exactly why he was wanted back in New York, but he knew. When Stanley Filkins interviewed him he understood completely. Stanley wanted to know the details about Matthew Bardwell, as well as the substance that Albert found wrapped in the paper in Polly's bandbox.

On June 30, 1858 the trial was set to begin. Lorenzo Olcott had traveled to subpoena an additional witness the day of the trial. The task was put in charge of Olcott since Alvin Pease was to escort Polly Frisch from the jail to the Court House in Batavia during the length of the trial.

Court convened at 9:00 a.m., June 30, 1858, to begin the process of choosing a jury. Sheriff Pease brought Polly Frisch into court and led her to her seat by her counsel. She was wearing a black silk dress, black satin bonnet, a white shawl, and jet-black bracelets and necklace. A somber appearance emanated from her before the courtroom crowd. Her mood was as somber as her attire, exhibiting a calm and cool composure. The courthouse was packed with those who were required to attend and those who were merely curious. Women didn't normally take an interest in the proceedings of these types of things, but this trial was different. Several women, believed to be from the town of Alabama, were among the onlookers.

The June Session of the Court of Oyer & Terminer came before the Honorable Benjamin F. Greene, Justice of the Supreme Court; and Session Justices, John G. Bixby and William Bennett. The prosecution was conducted by District Attorney George Bowen, and assisted by Albert Sawin, Esquire of Buffalo. The legal duo of Wakeman & Bryan conducted the case for the defense. When the prisoner was seated and the courtroom was called to order, the charges were read out loud. "The People vs. Polly Frisch, indicted for the murder of her husband, Henry Hoag, in July 1856 by poison."

Jury selection began as each person was brought in front of the defendant, Polly Frisch, and were examined. George Bowen questioned prospective jurors as to their ability to find a verdict of guilty based on the evidence. A guilty verdict meant capital punishment. If convicted, Polly would hang by the neck until dead. Bowen wanted to make sure the jurors would be unbiased about the thought of condemning a woman to death in this manner.

Seth Wakeman's questions centered on the jury's ability not to be swayed by public gossip or any previously formed opinions. Up to this point the exact details of any evidence that was gathered had remained quiet, but murmurs and whispers could be heard from one end of the county to the other. It would be important to the defense of their client that the jurors left the scuttlebutt outside and relied on the evidence they intended to show to prove Polly's innocence.

With the goals of both sides established the jury was chosen and sworn in by half past ten that morning. The jury, all farmers, was as follows: William P. Dunlap, Oakfield; Sidney P. Huntington, Pembroke; James Kinsey, Darien; George B. Kemp, Batavia; Orren (or Warren) Putnam, Batavia; Porter Davis (or David), Bergen; Joseph D. Cutler, Pembroke; Sidney W. Butler, Bethany; John H. Wiggins, Stafford; James Sheldon, Pavilion; Daniel Clark, Oakfield; and Phillip Amidon, Pembroke. For obvious reasons, no one from the town of Alabama was chosen for jury duty.

The selection processes now complete, the twelve men took their seats in the jury box. George Bowen then gave his opening argument as to what the prosecution intended to show. It seemed that the exhumation of the bodies and Matthew Bardwell would be their first line of questioning. The testimony taken in the morning would set up the line of questioning for the witnesses in the afternoon.

The majority of the witnesses for the prosecution that were called on in the forenoon were the doctors and others that attended the various exhumations. Even Robert Almay, the Alabama Cemetery sexton, was called to the stand.

Reuben Warren gave his account as what had gone on at the cemetery. He also spoke of the secret letter Polly had sent to Matthew Bardwell immediately after Henry's death.

The district attorney next called Andrew Davis and questioned him on the night he stayed at the Hoag's before Henry's death.

Figure 12. Old Genesee County Court House (on right). Early 1900s. During the 1850s it also housed the Sheriff's Office, Surrogate Court, Treasurer, and the County Clerk's Office.

Photo courtesy of the Genesee County History Department.

"Sat up with Hoag all night previous to his death," Davis said. "The prisoner steeped up some herbs and gave it to him to drink. He made several efforts to vomit during the night but couldn't. He had spasms sometimes, and that if he had no more he thought he should recover."

But Henry didn't recover. He died the next day. Seth, on cross-examination, intended to stress that although Henry's death was sudden after he said he thought he would recover, that it had nothing to do with Polly.

Seth Wakeman asked Andrew Davis about Polly's care of Henry. Davis replied, "Mr. Hoag called for the herb drink; he told his wife in the night that he feared a spasm was coming on, and she went in the room and rubbed him about five minutes. He felt better for it. She laid on the lounge near his bed that night; got up often to wait on him. Discovered no lack of attention on her part." The testimony of Andrew Davis was for the most part in Polly's favor.

Coroner Robert Baker was on the stand for quite some time. Seth Wakeman on cross-examination, focused on Baker's stop at the Center with the seed box containing Henry's stomach, before going back to Batavia the day the bodies were exhumed. He also had kept it in his house over night. The defense was trying to show that the seed box might have been tampered with.

At first, the details of digging up bodies had the spectator's attention. There was a natural morbid curiosity about the whole affair. As each doctor took the stand, it began to get redundant. Dr. Nelson Horning, Dr. Holton Ganson, and Dr. Samuel Bateman all gave their account of what had happened during the autopsy of Henry Hoag.

Although the children were exhumed at the same time, it could not be brought up during this trial. The closest they came to mentioning it was to say that Henry's stomach was put in a separate compartment than those of the two children. If the jury and the crowd in the courtroom didn't know they cut open the children the same as Henry, they did now.

Dr. Bateman had a bit more to add to his testimony than the rest of the physicians. Samuel Bateman was asked about the day that Polly had bought the arsenic.

"The prisoner got arsenic of me six or eight weeks before her husband's death. She said she wanted it to kill mice and rats." Bateman went on to explain that the arsenic was put into a vial and clearly labeled arsenic.

When Bowen asked of the general health of Henry, Bateman replied, "He had no constitutional difficulties that I know of except for a year before his death. He was naturally an industrious man. I saw him on the Sabbath morning previous to his death; had not probably seen him before for several weeks."

Samuel continued his testimony by telling of the cultivator accident. "His wife said he was hurt with a cultivator while cultivating out corn; that it struck against a stone and hit him in the pit of the stomach, some two or three weeks before; she supposed the blow was the cause of his injury. She said he vomited blood soon after, and he had not been well since."

The district attorney was attempting to focus on Henry being well up until the time Polly purchased the arsenic, but it backfired. As soon as Bateman mentioned the accident that Henry had, it cast serious doubts as to the cause of Henry's sudden illness. The prosecution didn't attempt to go any further with the witness.

Because of the hour Judge Greene adjourned the trial for lunch. The morning session had been long with most of the testimony surrounding medical technicalities and procedures surrounding the exhumation. Dr. Bateman's testimony about the arsenic and Henry's accident had been the most interesting thus far to the spectators.

When court reconvened the crowd was even larger than it had been that morning. The number of women had increased as well. Sheriff Pease had provided a seat next to the witness stand during the morning session for the reporter for the *Genesee County Herald & Spirit of the Times.* Judge Greene objected to the situation going on any further and moved the reporter farther back in the courtroom. The judge may have had a feeling that his courtroom could quickly get out of hand if not kept in check.

Samuel Bateman was called back to the stand to be crossed-examined by Seth Wakeman. The room waited in anticipation to see what more was going to be said about the arsenic. Instead, once again the topic of the exhumations was brought up. After listening to this line of questioning all morning no doubt there were a few who were starting to nod off.

The question Seth asked next would surly cause their heads to jerk back to attention. Wakeman finally asked him about the day Polly came to his store to purchase the arsenic. He was trying to get Bateman to admit that there was no way he could remember all the people he sold arsenic to.

Bateman under oath testified, "I frequently sold arsenic; can't remember all to whom I have sold it too. Never sold [Henry] Hoag any arsenic; prisoner lived on the farm when she purchased the arsenic. She said her husband wished her to get it, got an ounce vial near full, labeled 'Arsenic Poison'; she had not got any arsenic of me before. She did not wish me to charge it, said she would pay for it in a few days."

Samuel Bateman was then asked about Polly's behavior towards her husband. Dr. Bateman responded, "When I visited Hoag previous to his death I saw no unusual appearance in the prisoner; no want of feeling or inattention towards her husband. I discovered nothing to indicate that she was not an affectionate wife."

Doctor Bateman was finally asked to step down from the stand. It was hard to tell if his testimony helped or hurt either the prosecution or the defense.

Both sides could perceive Dr. Bateman's testimony as in their favor. It would ultimately depend on what the jury's perception was.

Dr. Samuel Bateman most likely passed his wife in the isle as he left the witness stand, as Calista Bateman was the next witness to be called. The prosecution had very few questions to ask Calista. She was the person to answer the door the day that Polly went to Alabama Center the second time to purchase the arsenic.

Mrs. Bateman explained how Polly had told her the same story about the mice and rats, and that she had some arsenic but had either misplaced it or lost it.

Calista went on to say, "She said Mr. Hoag was opposed to her getting it from fear of an accident from it. She said she was going to put it on bread and butter and put it through the lath (the house was not plastered) so that the children could not get it. Sold her a small vial of arsenic, labeled 'Poison'. This was after Mrs. Hoag had bought arsenic from my husband."

So there it was. The jury now knew that Polly had purchased arsenic on two separate occasions, first from Dr. Bateman several weeks before Henry's death and again from Mrs. Bateman in June.

More doctors were called to the witness stand next. Dr. Oliver P. Clark testified to receiving the stomach of Henry Hoag from Coroner Robert Baker, and his delivery of the seed box to Professor George Hadley of the medical college in Buffalo.

The next witness to be called, however, would be tough for the defense to turn to their side. Professor George Hadley was summoned to take the stand. Although the courtroom had heard several witnesses testify about what was done on the corpse of Henry

Hoag, this would be different. This was the man who did the actual chemical tests.

The prosecution opened its questioning by asking Hadley his qualifications and what his duties were in regards to the internal organs. Hadley began, "I am a Professor of Practical Chemistry. I have practiced chemistry for over twenty years, and have taught chemistry for over ten years. Toxicological Chemistry has occupied much of my attention. Dr. Clark brought me a box containing the remains of what was purported to be a human stomach, which I made chemical analysis of, and completed the examination some time last February. They were parts of the viscera of the abdominal cavity, and a part of the intestines were so well preserved that I had to cut them open."

Professor Hadley had just verified what the other doctors had surmised. He presented to the jury several specimens of Henry's tissue. Hadley elaborated further in a scientific manner his methods for producing the chemical results supporting the finding of arsenic. He also stated that the quantity was probably small but it would be detected in all body tissues had it been taken in poisonous doses.

Hadley continued, "Can detect arsenic any length of time after death, but it is difficult to ascertain the amount when decomposition is so far advanced."

District Attorney Bowen then asked Hadley to elaborate on the symptoms of arsenic poisoning. "It would cause great distress and vomiting. From secondary effects, a burning sensation in the stomach, and great thirst," Hadley explained. "Soon dejections from the bowels takes place sometimes with blood, and could die of exhaustion after a few days or weeks. Two grains of arsenic might produce death - taken in small doses it would produce death in from a few hours to six or eight days. Vomiting, by throwing off a part of the arsenic would prolong the life."

Seth Wakeman's line of questioning for the defense would focus on the fact that the stomach could have been tampered with before Professor Hadley had it in his possession. Baker had taken it with him to several locations before the box was delivered. It went into Clark's possession before it even got to Hadley. Could someone have tampered with it between the time it was taken from Henry's body and the time Clark delivered it to Buffalo? It did travel through a lot of hands before the seed box landed in those of Hadley's.

Seth questioned the professor on the type of tissue he examined and if he could tell from it whether arsenic could have been added after death instead of before. Hadley replied, "No means of knowing if arsenic was administered during life. I could not say positively whether portion examined was part of the stomach or not. It may be vomited from the system before death so as not to appear throughout the system."

Professor George Hadley's testimony was finally over. Once again, it would be how the jury interpreted what Professor Hadley gave witness to as to whose side his testimony benefited.

The final witnesses who testified that day for the prosecution were James Gumaer and Eli Bickford. Both said that they had visited Henry Hoag right before his death to find him to be very sick. Each attested to the fact that Polly had shown them a picture of Matthew Bardwell, and that Polly said Henry had wanted Matthew to work up the shoe leather.

Eli, however, had more to add. "I watched with Mrs. Hoag the Saturday night before his death; his wife said he had a hard vomiting spell just before I came, threw up some blood. He had a spasm during the night, said he had a death like feeling in his stomach, also a burning sensation, he said nobody could tell how he felt; the spasm would sometimes last fifteen minutes; he could barely breathe when they left him; could lie in no other position than his back. He complained of thirst. Prisoner gave him some gruel during the night."

Eli had just verified what Professor Hadley had said were the symptoms of arsenic poison. When Eli Bickford continued, to the dismay of District Attorney Bowen, he would distract the jury away from death by poisoning.

"I saw him on July 10th and made a new bargain for his building which I rented," Eli said. "He told me this day that a cultivator had hit him in the breast."

George Bowen would now have to ask Bickford something to steer them away from that comment. Bowen brought up Polly's lover Matthew Bardwell.

Eli responded, "The next day after Hoag's death prisoner came to me and requested that I would prepare to leave the shop by the middle of October, that Hoag had requested that Bardwell should come and work up the leather that was left, and that Bardwell could board with her or at the tavern; Hoag had said if she behaved herself it could do no harm."

On cross-examination Seth Wakeman also asked about the cultivator accident, Henry's illness and Polly's care of her husband. Eli answered, "Prisoner remained in attendance upon her husband until two or three o'clock when she retired; did not see any want of attention toward deceased on her part."

It had been a long first day of court. Judge Greene adjourned until 9:00 a.m. the next morning. It was hard to tell at this point which way the case was going. On one hand Professor Hadley had expertly proved there was arsenic in the tissue he tested. On the other hand, doubts were raised on the tissue itself. Was it Henry's stomach? Was the arsenic in his body before he died? Was his illness even caused by arsenic poisoning or was it because of the cultivator accident?

Although Matthew Bardwell's name was brought up several times, nothing was mentioned that would indicate an intimate relationship going on between Matthew and Polly. So where was the motive for murder?

District Attorney George Bowen was saving his most important witness for the People for tomorrow. This person would be the first witness to take the stand and his testimony would be the most damaging to Polly Frisch. Albert Hoag, Polly's own son, would enter the witness box on behalf of the prosecution, to testify against his mother.

13

HENRY'S TRIAL - Albert's Story

The July 1st, Thursday morning session of the trial was cancelled. This time it was not because Polly Frisch was sick, but because Judge Benjamin Greene was. Court reconvened at 2:00 p.m. with some new rules. The judge had ordered that the gentlemen leave their tobacco at home and their feet off the tables. It would appear the judge was tightening down the liberties that were being taken. It was not meant to be entertainment for the media or spectators; this was a trial, and he wanted it treated as such.

The densely crowded courtroom, that contained even more women than the day before, was called to order. The prosecution must have expected a reaction from the jury to their first witness. The courtroom was shocked as District Attorney George Bowen called Albert Hoag to the stand. One could just imagine the gasps of surprise as each spectator leaned to the person next to them whispering things like, "Isn't that her son?" or, "Why, he's just a child! Is the boy going to testify against his own mother?"

Albert took his seat in the witness box and was sworn in. After the boy gave his name he was asked to tell about himself. Albert answered, "I was eleven years old last November; live with my Uncle Lyman Hoag in Michigan. I can read and am learning to write. Henry Hoag was my father."

Albert told the account of how his mother had sent him to get a bottle of brandy a day or two before his father died. He went on to describe the episode pertaining to the arsenic. Albert explained how his mother had told him it was Saleratus and that she put it in the brandy to sweeten it.

Albert went on, "I took down the paper from behind the clock after my Ma went out of the room and looked at it. It was white like flour, and glistened a little, it did not look like Salaeratus [sic], it was not a fine grain."

Bowen then asked Albert what he knew about the secret meeting between Matthew Bardwell and his mother.

"I went to Wheatville with my Ma before my Pa died. We went in the buggy, Ma and I together. She told my Pa she was going to Alabama Center. My Ma saw Matthew and told me not to tell my Pa. Matthew was at our house. I saw Matthew and my Ma in bed together in the daytime, twice before my Pa died," Albert said. "My Pa saw them and he and my Ma had a fuss about it. My Pa told Matthew that he must leave; he didn't leave for a good while. I knew nothing of him and Ma going away together."

It was now Wakeman's turn to question the witness. Albert's testimony was hurting the defense. Seth Wakeman had to be careful how he handled Albert. It was obvious that the boy did not like his mother one bit, and resented her for what she had done to his father, as well as his sisters. One can imagine the hush that fell over the courtroom as the spectators waited with anticipation, wondering what this witness would say next.

Seth Wakeman began by asking Albert general questions about the Hoag family and Matthew's place in it. Unfortunately for Seth, he would not succeed in getting any testimony from Albert that would help his client. In fact, his continued questioning only added to the vision of Polly being an evil woman.

The closest Seth came to helping Polly was getting Albert to admit that he didn't care much about his mother. The comment Albert made about not liking her any better then, than he did now, was not a normal feeling for a child to express when talking about his mother. Seth hoped the jury saw that Albert's poor opinion of Polly might induce him to lie. The question still remained, if Polly had not done anything wrong than why would Albert dislike her so much?

Wakeman continued to cross-examine Polly's son, but he should have left the subject of Matthew Bardwell alone. Polly's counsel tried to show that Henry and Matthew were friends and that Matthew was accepted as one of the family. Albert began by admitting it was true that Matthew Bardwell had lived in their home as one of the family; but immediately elaborated further on his mother's and Matthew's affair.

The subject Albert spoke of before he left the witness box stunned the courtroom. It would be hard to believe that the words were to come out of the mouth of a child, in a very blunt and direct manner. There was a stir in the courtroom as Albert continued to reveal even more shocking and damaging testimony against his mother, things that were not spoken of back then.

"Bardwell lived in our family, and worked for father at the time Bardwell and Ma were in bed together," said Albert. "He worked at shoemaking in my Pa's shop."

Albert went on to explain what his father's reaction had been after he told his father about the first time that he caught his mother and Matthew together.

"The house is close by the shop. Pa went in and I went with him. We went in the bedroom; the door was opened. Pa went to the bedroom door first; I followed. It was in the summertime," Albert said. "No curtain. Matthew's clothes were on; he was lying on the outside of the bed, Ma was lying down. They were in bed when Pa went out. Pa talked to Matthew after he saw them in bed; it was in the shop that he talked to him."

As Albert had previously testified, his parents fought over it, but Matthew ultimately stayed with the Hoags. Albert wasn't finished yet, however. During his questioning by the prosecution, Albert had not gone into detail about the second encounter. He was about to now.

"I saw them in bed again when Pa was in Medina," Albert began. "It was in warm weather; the door was not opened. We all slept in that bedroom. They were lying down on the bed when I came in. They said nothing to me nor I to them. Pa came home that night. I told him when he came home all that I had seen. Think Matthew was in bed when Pa came home; think he did not go to work that day; but he worked in the shop after that. I did not hear Pa talk to him again."

Seth changed the topic to that of Henry's cultivator accident. Albert only briefly discussed his father's injury. He had been with his father that day, and did not recall his father being injured that badly. Albert did remember his father spitting up blood the night before he died. He also recalled it was Dr. Townsend's idea for Polly to administer brandy to Henry. Albert told the court how his mother had given him the bottle in which to get it.

Maybe Seth Wakeman wanted the jury to see it had been the doctor's idea to administer brandy to Henry. Once again, Seth left the door open for Albert. The boy proceeded to tell the court exactly what Polly did with the bottle of brandy once she got a hold of it.

"Saw my Ma take a paper from behind the clock which had white powder in it, and put it in the brandy. There was no one else in the room when she did it. The substance in the paper was as much as a blade of a knife would hold. She turned the stuff out from the paper into the bottle; there was a very little left. I was close to her when she put it in. She put the paper back again. The bottle was a good sized one," Albert testified. "Don't know how full it was. She shook it up. Nobody was in the room when she went in where Pa was. Pa drank it from the bottle; she held it to his mouth. Pa said nothing, drank a little of it, said he didn't wish her to give him any more of it for it made him worse. I don't know what she did with the bottle."

Seth Wakeman hadn't handled this boy in any way that would help his client. His only hope now was to try and discredit Albert's testimony. Wakeman tried to force Albert to say he had been primed by his Uncle Lyman Hoag to tell the version he just told the jury. Polly's son stuck to his story.

"Lime Hoag came down with me, they wrote for me to come. He did not say what for," Albert said. "I knew what I came down for. I told Lyman first about the paper when I was in Michigan; don't know how long I had been there before I told Lime. I first mentioned it. I have talked to Stanley Filkins about it here. [I] have not talked with anyone else. Lime wanted me to swear to what I knew and no more."

The testimony of Albert Hoag was finished. The boy had stuck to his guns about what he felt to be the truth. Despite being on the witness stand for an agonizing amount of time and badgered by the defense, he did not waiver from his account of the events.

In the *Rochester Democrat's* report of the trial, which was also printed in the *LeRoy Gazette*, they relayed the following observation of Albert's testimony:

> The witness sustained a searching cross-examination without varying materially from his testimony on the direct examination, although sick with the measles and evidently quite feeble; [he said] his mother carried the bottle into the bedroom and gave his father some after she put the powder into it; a little while after that his father said he didn't want any more of the brandy, as it made him worse. The excitement was intense in the Courtroom during the examination of this witness, and everyone felt that it bore heavily against the prisoner.

When Albert stepped down from the stand the room was buzzing with what had just happened. Judge Greene managed to bring the courtroom back to order so the next witness could be called to testify. One after another the residents of the town of Alabama would be called to the stand. The prosecution called Selah Vosburg.

Selah would tell of the day he saw Henry in his illness, but it was much the same as the other witnesses had been. He did mention that it was Polly who said Henry had cholera morbus not Henry himself.

Selah was asked about his appraisal of the Hoag property in Alabama Center. He told how Polly insisted that the leather and shoe making supplies not be sold because she wanted Matthew Bardwell to make up the leather. Nothing of any interest was elicited on cross-examination. Selah Vosburg, like some of the other witnesses for the prosecution, attested to Polly's care of her husband.

Selah said, "I saw nothing in the prisoner's conduct, while there, which was suspicious."

James Espy was called to the stand next. He told the jury how half an hour after Henry died, and before his body was even laid out, Polly asked him if he knew of any one to buy the horse, oxen and yoke. She also wanted the hay cut so it could be sold.

Espy, on cross, also made a similar statement to that of Selah Vosburg. "I saw nothing on her part like inattention to the deceased when I was to see him before his death."

The prosecution had only a few witnesses left to call. George Lester, the husband of Polly's sister Elizabeth, would also testify against her. His testimony would be almost as shocking as Albert's had been.

When Bowen asked George Lester about the argument between Polly and Henry going to the farm he answered, "She was opposed to going there; said she would not go down there, and if she did she would kill him. She said, 'I vow I will!' She seemed to be angry at the time she said she would take his life. I told Eli Horning about the confession of Mrs. Hoag about two months before I was sworn in Alabama."

Figure 13. Courtroom inside the old Court House, relatively unchanged, where Polly Frisch was tried for murder.

Photo courtesy of the Genesee County History Department.

Imagine the gasps of horror that swept the room when George Lester told the court that Polly vowed she would kill Henry. George wasn't finished yet, however. There was still the matter of the arsenic tainted brandy.

George Lester testified to drinking some brandy from a small bottle. He continued, "[The] prisoner and I gave him the brandy from a tumbler. Gave him a tablespoon at a time. Hoag said the brandy hurt him. The brandy in the tumbler was a lighter color than the one in the bottle. There were other bottles of brandy, one larger and one smaller."

When George Lester was cross-examined by the defense about how Polly treated her husband, he answered, "I'm not exactly friendly towards the prisoner. I saw nothing unkind on her part towards her husband that night."

Mrs. Filkins, Stanley's mother was sworn in next, and then Mrs. Barber. They both testified to the same thing—that Polly had told them that Henry would not live long if he stayed on the farm.

Mrs. Barber also told the court what Polly had said about the fortuneteller's prediction, "I saw prisoner after Hoag's death. She said to me, 'What did I tell you! There has been one.' The child was then sick. Last fall I saw a paper in the prisoner's band box, which she said contained arsenic."

Both women gave testimony that did not reflect well on Polly. The story Delia Avery and Mrs. Potter told was similar to the last witnesses. Polly had told both these women as well, that if Henry moved to the farm he would not live six months and she did not care if Henry died. Polly was sorry she got married and wished she were clear of her husband and children. The more they spoke about what Polly had told them the worse it was getting for Polly.

The afternoon session wasn't going well for the defense. There were too many people that Polly had been overly verbal with about her feelings towards her husband and children. The best Seth Wakeman could do was wait until it was his chance to call witnesses on behalf of his client.

Witness upon witness from Alabama took the stand and trampled Polly's character into the ground. Lovina Tabor and Lucinda Farley each spoke of Polly going on about Matthew Bardwell right after her husband Henry's death. When the last two witnesses testified, it was icing on the cake of the prosecution.

With the women still fanning themselves from the shock of the previous testimonies, George Bowen called Timothy Hoag to the stand. George asked Timothy to elaborate on the day he came from Michigan to visit his brother Henry in Alabama Center before the move to the farm.

"She said she would not go there," replied Timothy. "Henry said he would go and take the children. She said if he did she would not go, she said if she could not get rid of him in any other manner she would kill him and she would come back to the shop and have Matthew in the shop."

The stir in the courtroom had gotten progressively louder with each witness who testified to Polly's comments of her desire to murder her husband. Bowen was getting exactly the reaction he had hoped for. Before he rested his case, he recalled one witness back to the stand. He wanted to leave no doubt in the jury's mind as to how Henry came to his death.

For his last witness District Attorney Bowen recalled Dr. Oliver P. Clark, who was also a druggist. He asked him not what the regular symptoms of arsenic poisoning were but what they would be upon an overdose.

Clark responded, "If a person should be sick and die with the symptoms attendant upon Hoag's death, they would be the same as to follow an overdose of arsenic; and if arsenic were found in the stomach of a patient dying with those symptoms, there would be no reasonable doubt that death was caused by arsenic."

With that said, and no re-cross, the prosecution rested its case. Court adjourned until two o'clock Friday afternoon.

The day's session was a fatal blow to the defense. The district attorney had out done himself. There was little doubt that Polly's own neighbors did not think very much of her. When in front of them, during Henry's illness, she looked like the loving and attentive wife. Behind closed doors, however, and in anger in front of others, she did not mince words about her scorn for her husband and children. She had vocalized, to far too many people, her desire to see Henry dead.

It would be hard for Seth Wakeman to undo the damage that had been done. The majority of the people that knew Polly had testified against her. The only witness from Alabama that would testify in her defense, other than her sister Julia Maybach and her father Schubel Franklin, was J.S. McComb. It did not look good at all for Polly Frisch.

14

HENRY'S TRIAL – The Verdict

On Friday, promptly at 2:00 p.m., court reconvened as William G. Bryan took the floor. A change in strategy had taken place. William was to handle the questioning for the Friday afternoon session. The *Republican Advocate* newspaper included the following observation in an article printed in the July 6th edition:

> W.G. Bryan, Esq. made the opening plea on the part of the defense. It was characterized by power and eloquence, and was listened to by a large audience, in the most breathless attention. The address evidently made a deep impression upon all the courthouse.

A good opening argument may have helped, but there were no strong witnesses to back up his speech. The first witness Bryan called to the stand was Polly's father, Schubel Franklin. Schubel was asked about Matthew Bardwell. His answer was a short one. He said yes, he knew him. He was Henry's apprentice, and he moved to Canada to do his work. That was it. Schubel told his account of Henry's illness and the doctor's treatment, but nothing dramatic. William then asked Schubel what he knew about Polly and Henry's intimate relationship. He needed desperately to show the jury that the couple acted like a normal husband and wife.

Schubel began, "Hoag moved on my farm in April, 1856. I rented him the farm for three years. While at the farm Hoag and Polly lodged together sometimes. Sometimes Henry slept with me, especially after he had been working hard; and he preferred doing so to being obliged to take care of the children. Saw them in bed together a short time before going on the farm. I never saw any lack of attention on her part towards her husband."

Nothing of interest was gathered on cross-examination. There was really no point. After all the other witnesses had testified to the poor relationship between Henry and Polly her father's testimony was moot. After all, he was trying to defend his daughter. What else was he supposed to say?

Schubel was dismissed from the stand without further questioning. The defense called Julia Maybach, Polly's youngest sister. Julia was only 15 at the time of the murders, and age 17 during Henry's trial. Polly and Julia were always very close. Her testimony would be as biased as her father Schubel's had been. Unfortunately, Wakeman & Bryan had no one else to call to the stand in Polly's defense.

Julia began her testimony. "I was at her house a good deal of the time during the last year of his life. I knew Matthew Bardwell; he worked for Hoag. Bardwell went to Canada. Hoag went to Medina with him and when he returned, he brought Bardwell's daguerreotype with him and showed it to me. This was a short time before they moved on the farm."

Despite what Albert had testified to, Julia insisted that Matthew had gone with Henry to Medina and not alone. She was trying to discredit Albert's testimony on catching his mother and Matthew in bed together while Henry had been gone.

Why would Henry care to show off Matthew's picture?

Julia continued, "In June, before his death, I heard Hoag ask Polly to go to Dr. Bateman's to get some arsenic."

According to Julia, Polly did not want to get it. Julia said Polly went to get the arsenic like Henry requested, and came back more than two hours later. The rest he left in the paper and placed it on top of the closet. Julia continued her version, placing Polly outside, which implied that Polly didn't know where Henry put it.

The defense shifted to the line of questioning about Henry's last days. "Albert was sent for brandy the night before Henry died. This was before sundown. I saw him when he returned," Julia said. "He had a bottle with brandy in it. He handed it to me and I laid it on the stand."

Both Albert and Julia agreed that it was Albert who went for the brandy; however, the time element was wrong. Julia was not there when Albert got back from Hescock's with the brandy. Albert said he had handed the bottle directly to Polly upon his return. By sundown George Lester had arrived and Albert was already well on his way to get Andrew Davis, not on his way to get the brandy. Julia attempted to cast doubts on Albert's testimony, as well as George Lester's and Andrew Davis'. She did her best to try and prove that Polly did not have possession of the bottle while alone.

Julia next elaborated on Dr. Townsend's medical treatment of Henry. Dr. Townsend had moved to Michigan and could not be located to testify himself. Nothing new was elicited from Julia's description of the medicine that was administered. Julia went on to tell about the conversation she overheard of Henry's request to have Matthew Bardwell take over after his death.

Once again we must point out that no one else, during the many days of Henry's illness, heard anything of the kind. Henry told no one else this, and no one else ever overheard the comment either. Eli Bickford and Henry Hoag had been very good friends. If Henry were to ask anyone to take over the shop it would have been Eli, not his wife's ex-lover.

Julia continued by re-telling the story of the fortuneteller and her prediction. When cross-examined by George Bowen on this subject Julia answered, "Think the fortune telling was taken as joke. I never saw any more arsenic in the house than that purchased at Hoag's request. Think I saw father drink out of the brandy bottle four or five weeks after Hoag's death."

Julia's testimony did not help Polly's case. Polly herself had retold the fortune teller's prediction, as if it were true, to many people. In mentioning her father drinking the brandy weeks later, she might have been implying that there was nothing wrong with it. Her testimony was as weak as her father's had been.

In all fairness, these were the two people that loved Polly the most. They may have truly believed she was innocent. If that were the case, since so many witnesses had given such damaging testimony, they may have thought she was being railroaded. Knowing that a guilty verdict meant she would be hung, they would have said anything in order to try and save her. If Polly told them she didn't do it, they would believe her based on love alone. Love can be blind, and Polly had a persuasive personality. It is very easy for that type of person to convince someone of almost anything.

The stress that this whole affair put on Julia and Schubel must have been horrifying. A woman had never been hung for murder before in the county of Genesee. They did not want their beloved Polly to be the first. Julia was also testifying under duress. She was pregnant with her first child. She was only a few months along but the trial was already affecting her health.

William Bryan didn't have much further to go in the defense of his client. The only other witness they had, that knew Henry when he was alive, was summoned to the stand. J.S. McComb of Alabama was sworn in and began his testimony.

"I live in Alabama. I knew Henry Hoag. I bargained with him the first of July to rent the farm, on which he lived, was to take possession in the fall. Had made no writings but was to do so. Hoag was going to move back to his old place." This was the extent of McComb's testimony.

We believe that this question was asked to cast doubts over the alleged arguments about living on the farm. Henry was planning to move back, and Polly knew this. There would be no reason to fight in front of others about living there if they were moving back anyway. If Polly and Henry weren't really at each other's throats, why would she want to kill him? The defense was trying to show the jury that they weren't the bickering couple at all.

It was a good thing for Polly that the child born after Henry's death was never mentioned. If the time of the baby's birth had been compared to the other testimony, the question would have been raised as to whose child it was. George Bowen could have implied that the child was really Matthew Bardwell's. The prosecution would have been able to show the jury a very good motive for murder.

William called two doctors to the stand as his own expert witnesses on the symptoms of arsenic poisoning and its effects on human tissue, Dr. C.W. Griswold and Dr. John Cotes. Dr. Griswold, who had been a physician and surgeon for over thirteen years, focused on the fact that if poisoning was the case, other medicines should have been administered. Griswold wasn't disputing the possibility of Henry being poisoned at this point. He was disputing whether it was the cause of his death. Dr. Griswold was implying, in a subtle manner, that the doctor had prescribed the wrong medicine.

Next, William Bryan raised the question if Henry had been poisoned at all. Griswold began, "We often find extreme nausea and depression in diseases of the bowels, in typhoid fever, intermittent and bilious fever, also in hemorrhage. Spasms are produced by irritations of the nervous system. Spasms often preceded death from any cause. Internal hemorrhage of the stomach would produce vomiting."

Griswold tried to show that there were other possibilities that may have caused Henry's death, including an injury caused by a blow to the stomach from a cultivator.

Lastly for the defense was Dr. John Cotes, Polly's physician while in jail. Cotes explained the effects of arsenic poisoning the same as the doctors for the prosecution had, and then some. He mentioned spasms, convulsions, blistering and swelling around the mouth. He went on to explain that the symptoms of cholera morbus resemble arsenic. While the prosecution tried to show that everyone at the time thought Henry had cholera when he was really being poisoned, the defense on the other hand, stated just the opposite. Dr. Cotes' conclusion was that even though the prosecution said Polly poisoned her husband, what he really died of was cholera.

William Bryan succeeded in creating doubts as to Henry Hoag's cause of death. There was no one else to call; no one else in Alabama was willing to testify to save Polly Frisch. Although the defense team of Wakeman & Bryan had tried their best, there was nothing else to do but rest their case. They had started well with their opening argument, and ended well by calling their own experts to the stand. It was everything in between, and the strong case that the prosecution presented that worried them. The trial was to reconvene at eight o'clock the next morning. Seth Wakeman would give the closing arguments on behalf of the defense. William and his partner didn't think they had a chance in hell of saving their client from the hangman's noose.

Figure 14. Old Court House as it looks today. (Still in use. New Court Building in background, right.) ***Photo by C. Amrhein.***

Court reconvened promptly at eight o'clock on Saturday morning July the 3rd. It had been a long two days, but it was almost over. Soon Seth Wakeman and William Bryan would know if they had saved their client or condemned her to death. The courtroom was on pins and needles. Almost all of the spectators felt she was guilty, but what did the jury think?

For the People, Mr. Swain Esq. of Buffalo was asked to sum up the reasons why the jury should find Polly Frisch guilty of murder in the first degree for the death of her husband Henry. The *Republican Advocate* said he, "... addressed the jury in an impressive manner."

Seth Wakeman's closing statement lasted four hours. This was their last chance. Seth took every opportunity he had left to speak as long as he needed. The same newspaper said, "The case was eloquently summed up on the part of the defense", and Judge Benjamin Greene was said to have been "very able and impartial" in giving his directions to the jury.

At three o'clock in the afternoon the jurors finally left the courtroom to deliberate. They were only gone a short time when they returned and rendered their verdict.

"Not guilty," read the foreman.

One by one the jury was poled. It was true. The jury had found Polly Frisch innocent of the murder of her husband. The courtroom was in chaos. This is not what was expected to happen by any means.

The *Rochester Democrat* reported, "There appeared to be no doubt on the part of the spectators or the jury of the guilt of the prisoner, but the evidence did not warrant a conviction."

First there was the conflicting testimony on the effects of arsenic. Second was the fact that Henry did have an accident that may have caused an internal injury. It didn't matter if they got along or that she was having an affair. They could not say for sure, beyond a shadow of a doubt, that Polly had murdered her husband Henry Hoag.

The *Advocate* reported, "During the summing up by the prosecution Mrs. Frisch maintained a bold and unflinching countenance, not withstanding the many pointed allusions to her conduct towards her paramour, as brought out in the evidence of her son."

Polly was immediately returned to jail. She would now have to be tried on one of the other indictments. Would it be for the death of Eliza Jane or for Frances? The prosecution needed time to prepare. They would need to contact Professor George Hadley post haste and ask him which would be the stronger case. George Bowen had to prosecute the case of the child whose body contained the most poison. If it was only a minimal amount it could be said to have come from medicine prescribed, accidentally, or put in after the stomachs were taken from the bodies.

It was not enough to say that there was arsenic present in the corpses. In order to convict Polly Frisch, Bowen needed to know how much. They needed to know if there was a large enough amount in any of the Hoag children to be considered unusual. More testing would need to be done. Professor Hadley would once again be asked to take upon the gruesome task of handling the remains of Henry's daughters. This time they did not want any doubt in the minds of the jurors. He wanted them to be able to see that the only way a large amount of arsenic got into the bodies of the children is if Polly put it there.

Polly's father and sister Julia were no doubt elated. Although this was good news, the whole situation seemed hopeless. They still had to prosecute Polly for the other murders. Julia was in turmoil over the whole thing. It saved her sister from the gibbet a little longer, but the ordeal of going through another trial, testifying once more, being interrogated again by the prosecution, it was too horrible to imagine.

Before two weeks had passed Julia went into premature labor. It was believed to be caused by the stress of the trials. The first child of Julia and William Maybach was born in the town of Alabama on July 15, 1858. Charles, as they would name him, was so small that his size was compared to that of a quart jar. In those days, the odds of a child living who was born premature were slim. The one good thing that would come out of those terrible months of anguish was that their son Charles would live—he would be crippled—but he would live. It was a happy occasion, and a blessing for a family that had experienced so much death.

15

TRIAL FOR ELIZA JANE

There were four prisoners in the Genesee County Jail during the incarceration of Polly Frisch in the summer of 1858. Polly was the only female. Sheriff Alvin Pease gave reporter L.A. Baker of the *Republican Advocate* a tour of the jail, which they printed in their August 24, 1858 issue:

> It gives us pleasure to state that I found it clean and in order, and apparently in as good condition as could be expected of such an institution. The prisoners, four in number (one female), were clean and healthy in their appearance, and every precaution is taken for their safekeeping. A portion of the jail of the west side including the upper tier of cells, is partitioned off, for the reception of female prisoners. This includes all the windows on that side of the house; consequently the male department of the prison is not sufficiently ventilated. A window near the northwest corner, permitting a current of air to pass through is greatly needed for the health and comfort of the prisoners.

The reporter was allowed to examine the jail records during his visit. Of the 135 people that had been imprisoned over the last six months, Polly was the only one held on the charge of murder. There is an interesting correlation between crimes and alcohol that seems to be timeless. Out of the 135 inmates, 106 were in jail due to drunkenness or crimes committed while drunk.

L.A. Baker made the following comment in his article which society still debates. “It would be a curious and interesting inquiry, to know how much cost was made in each of these cases, and also the amount of jail fees and board, but this part of the subject is left, for an intelligent and tax-paying public to pursue.”

By the time the Frisch cases were through, it would cost the county several thousands of dollars. By the standards of the day it would be considered an astronomical amount of money to house and convict one person.

Nevertheless, the county allotted a large amount in its budget for the necessities of their prisoners. They were provided with clothing and boots or shoes as needed. The jail itself was well maintained. We found several receipts for brooms, wood for the stove, and building supplies to make repairs. There were receipts showing that new sheets, blankets, and ticking were purchased often for the cells; even tobacco was purchased for those who smoked. One receipt showing a purchase from Smith & Sons, dated December 11, 1857, was for a looking glass. This would appear to be the type of item that would be purchased for the use of a woman. All in all, the prisoners were well cared for and housed in a clean environment.

As Polly sat in her cell awaiting her next court date, the prosecution was prepared for the next trial. Eli P. Vail, constable from the town of Alabama, was subpoenaing witnesses. Meanwhile, District Attorney George Bowen was impatiently waiting to hear some news from Professor Hadley on his latest testing. During late summer Hadley was away in Vermont lecturing at the colleges there, which was his habit to do that time of year.

On the 24th of August, George Hadley received a letter at Castletown, Vermont, where he was staying. The letter was from District Attorney Bowen inquiring as to the analysis on the remains of the two children. He wished to know, of the two remaining cases, which one would his evidence be the most undisputed and direct. Hadley did not have his notes with him in Vermont, but sensed that Bowen desired an immediate answer. Hadley penned out his expert opinion, shown below, and mailed it back the same day:

> Castletown, Vermont Aug. 24, 1858
> Geo Bowen
> Dear Sir
>
> Of the one child, Dr. Clark brought no stomach, but a bit of intestine. That contained a large (comparatively) amount of arsenic and my testing would be perfectly positive & beyond being quibbled at. The name of the child I do not now remember, but Dr. Clark can give it to you.
>
> In the stomach of the other child there was only the slightest trace & hardly discoverable & although I feel pretty well convinced in my own mind, I should not testify so strongly & there would be some chance to throw doubt

on the conclusions. By all means, take the other case.

I am engaged now for a little more than 3 weeks then in Middlebury till the 24th of November; after that I shall be in Buffalo during the winter. If the trial could be put along a little it would save the county some expense & myself a good deal of inconvenience.

Yours Truly
George Hadley

The trouble was Bowen didn't want to wait. He began to prepare for November's Circuit Court anyway. Upon reading the letter from Professor Hadley, it appeared that the best case to try was the murder of Eliza Jane. Hadn't she been the one with the bit of intestines? Perhaps Clark verified that Hadley was referring to Eliza Jane. Remember, all the doctors had admitted that they were not sure which of the internal organs they were taking. It was only a guess. Hadley did not have his notes with him in Vermont at the time he answered George Bowen's letter. In actuality, the professor was not talking about Eliza Jane's body as having a large amount of arsenic, but Frances'. George Bowen's haste to prepare for trial would be costly.

It was now October and Professor Hadley felt it was time to bill the county for his services. He had already provided George Bowen with enough to present his case. On the sixth of the month, Hadley wrote up his bill for the analysis he had performed on the Hoag's. In his mind all the testing that was needed had been done on all of the victims. Once again, he asked the county to please wait until he returned from Vermont before scheduling the case for trial.

In his bill, he added a paragraph that in part read, "I close my labors here on the 24th of Nov. You must try to put off this case some way till after that, for I am really afraid my employers will absolutely refuse me leave of absence this time. Indeed they can not spare me anyway as I can see."

Hadley charged the county fifty dollars each for analyzing the body parts of Henry Hoag, Frances Hoag, Eliza Jane Hoag, and the stomach of an infant child. Also, ten dollars for analyzing the contents of a snuffbox, as Hadley referred to it, suspected to contain arsenic. His fee was very low in comparison to the normal charge for such a task. In his letter he felt it was worth commenting that it had been a distasteful and inconvenient undertaking. Professor Hadley wrote the following in his bill:

> The bodies had been buried many months, & the stomachs were consequently in an exceedingly decayed and offensive condition. It is not easy to explain to the Board in writing the great labor involved in these most difficult & disagreeable & impossible of all chemical investigations. The time and travel necessary occupied in attending Court ought really to be taken into the account. This has already occupied between one and two weeks & has required journal making and a total of 1600 miles.

In other words, the county was getting off cheap considering what the Court had expected of him.

Despite the professor's second request to wait until his return from Vermont, the preparations for the case continued as planned. The jury's list had been prepared a month ago for November's session of Circuit Court. Things progressed smoothly for the prosecution. At the beginning of November everything was in place. Eight Constables had been sworn in to assist with court duties for the month. They were Lester H. Gould, Charles Sprague, R. B. Pease, Oliver Parrish, L.H. Olcott, S.F. Moore, Fredrick Oswald, and Eli P. Vail.

Their duties were the same as usual, to subpoena witnesses and bring them to court when it was time, and to bring the prisoners to court. During the month of November there were twelve men in the jail along with Polly Frisch. Three were in for larceny, one for rape and the others were awaiting sentencing. Once again, Polly was the only person being held on the charge or murder.

Stanley Filkins, as usual, was helping the prosecution with its case. He would spend three days in preparation for the trial. This was added to his bill to the county. Bowen was ready as well. The only problem was that the prosecuting attorney had only three witnesses to call to the stand. We can assume that two of the witnesses were the men who had given testimony during the inquest that was held almost a year ago. The other witness would be Professor George Hadley. George Bowen was hoping that Hadley's testimony would be strong enough to convict Polly Frisch for the murder of her daughter Eliza Jane.

Despite Hadley's wishes, and the cost to the county to bring him from Vermont, he was summoned to Genesee County by court order for the trial that was scheduled for November 10th. Hadley gathered his specimens and notes and boarded the train that would take him to Batavia, New York. On the long journey Professor Hadley studied his notations and prepared to testify in the case of Frances Hoag.

Professor Hadley arrived at the courthouse at 4:00 p.m. on the 10th, only to discover he was prepared for the wrong trial. By the time he realized his mistake, it was too late. There was no time for Professor Hadley to confer with the district attorney before the trial began. While Hadley thought he was to be called to testify on the large amount of arsenic in the body of Frances, George Bowen was getting ready to question the professor on the amount of poison in the remains of Eliza Jane. Hadley would have to answer honestly, although the outlook for success was not good.

Judge Noah Davis, Supreme Court Justice, was presiding over the current trial. John G. Bixby and William Barnett, were the Session Justices; H.W. Hascall, Clerk; and Robert Baker, Crier.

It took much longer this time to select a jury. Alternate jurors had to be called. *The Genesee County Herald* reported in their November 13th issue, "This jury was obtained under great disadvantage. The panel having been exhausted before the required number was obtained; Court ordered the Sheriff to summons five Talismen. It was with the greatest difficulty that jurors were found who had not formed an opinion, thereby becoming incompetent."

The jurors selected for this trial were: William Bradey, Elba (Foreman); Cyrus Phelps, Pembroke; Charles Moreau, Batavia; Thomas Wiggins, Stafford; Cyrus F. Starks, Elba; J.L. Johnson, Stafford; Solomon Shoulters, Batavia; Ezra F. Coleman,

Pembroke; H.E. Parker, Elba; John Brown, Oakfield; and William E. Covill, Pavilion.

Polly Frisch was composed and smiling as Sheriff Alvin Pease brought her into the courtroom. She certainly did not give the appearance of someone who had killed her own child. Robert Baker called the court to order as the prosecution got ready to present its case. George Bowen did not have much of a case to present. He called the first two witnesses but their testimony was nothing of any importance, definitely not anything to convict a person of murder. Professor George Hadley was then called to the stand.

Bowen thought that the professor's testimony about the large amount of arsenic that he had found would clinch his case. The district attorney began to question the professor on the remains of Eliza Jane. There was nothing Hadley could do. He had to give his response on his findings of Eliza Jane. Hadley replied to Bowen's question.

"I can not positively swear that there was arsenic in the stomach of Eliza Jane Hoag," answered Professor Hadley.

Bowen was stunned. What was going on? As soon as the prosecutor realized what had happened, he threw up his hands in disgust with no further questions. The defense really had nothing to defend. The prosecution hadn't proved a thing. Wakeman and Bryan were satisfied to rest their case as well. Due to the late hour, the Judge adjourned court for the day.

George Bowen immediately pulled Professor Hadley aside to discuss what had just transpired in the courtroom. Hadley explained that he did not have his notes with him in Vermont. In his mind he had confused the body parts of the children. He had really meant Frances Hoag and not Eliza Jane Hoag in his letter. In order for the district attorney to take immediate action after the trial ended, he would need the professor's help before he left town again. George Hadley wrote up an affidavit explaining the entire events of what had happened from the day that he first received the letter from the district attorney. Now they would have to wait to see what would happen tomorrow.

The next morning Polly Frisch was once again brought into court to face her peers. Closing arguments were given quickly by each side. Both the defense and the prosecution were sure which way the jury would decide. Before the jurors left the room to deliberate, Judge Noah Davis reminded them that they had to believe there was sufficient evidence in order to render a verdict of guilty. The jurors conferred without even leaving the jury box.

The Forman rose to read the jury's decision. "Not guilty," declared Foreman Bradley.

As with the last trial, Polly was swiftly escorted back to the jail by Sheriff Pease.

District Attorney George Bowen immediately wrote a Motion to the Court relating the error in communication between Hadley and himself. Bowen expressed his desire to proceed with prosecuting Polly Frisch for the murder of her daughter Frances Hoag. This time he wanted more time to prepare. He did not want to repeat the same mistake again. In Bowen's own words, the following is taken from the Motion to the Court to postpone the next trial:

> Deponent says that he prepared the said case of Eliza Jane for trial in good faith & did not know of the mistake of said Hadley until his arrival here at the

> Court House about 4 p.m. yesterday while said trial was in progress when Dr. Hadley informed deponent himself of the mistake which he had made. And this deponent further says that it is impossible to prepare the case upon the other indictment for trial this term a portion of the witnesses residing out of the county of Genesee & one residing in the State of Michigan. That the reason why the case was not in readiness for trial this term is that the deponent did not intend to try this indictment because of the intimation in Prof. Hadley's letter of the weakness & uncertainness of his evidence in the case.
>
> Signed George Bowen

Bowen explained that the weakness of the evidence really had applied to the case of Eliza Jane and not the case of Frances. The witness from Michigan he was referring to was of course, Albert Hoag. Albert was living in Michigan at the time of Eliza Jane's death so he was not needed for that trial. He would, however, be an important witness in the case for the murder of his sister Frances.

With Professor George Hadley's affidavit attached to his motion to the court, he filed his documents with the court on Friday the 12th of November. Bowen hoped that the Court would understand and make allowances for the need to delay his prosecution of Polly on the murder of Frances Hoag. This would be the last case of the People vs. Polly Frisch, or so he thought. The district attorney would soon find out that he was wrong.

16

FRANCES – Trial No. 1

Although she always appeared in court smiling and showed no outward appearance of anxiety, something was medically unsound about Polly Frisch. Unfortunately, there are no detailed records on her medical condition. To be so chipper after being on trial twice already for murder does not seem to be normal behavior. Maybe she did not grasp the scope of the situation she was in. We feel confident that she was suffering from some sort of mental instability.

Dr. John Cotes visited Polly on December 1st, possibly for a routine visit before the next trial. By mid-December, however, Dr. Cotes was back at the jail attending to Polly on a daily basis. From the 14th to the 19th the doctor had been called to the jail to treat her reoccurring illness. In comparing her court dates and Dr. Cote's medical log we ruled out Polly's behavior in court as being drug induced. Polly was not being treated or given any kind of medication during the first two trials, nor on any days in close proximity to those trials. Whatever caused her to display detachment from the situation was something within Polly herself.

Sheriff Alvin Pease was busy serving thirty-five subpoenas. Constable Lester Gould had traveled to Springwater, NY to serve a subpoena on someone, whose identity is unknown, in relation to the Frisch case. The same people who testified for the prosecution at the trial for the murder of Henry were subpoenaed to testify at the trial for the murder of Frances, plus there were other witnesses listed in expense reports. Some of them were not required to testify or we do not have the documentation of their testimony. Just so we account for the historical facts, they were: Mr. and Mrs. James Eaton, Mrs. Vorman, H. Bunce, and those with the last names of Roff, Winchell, Laughlin, Green, and Tyler. The latter might very well have been one of the Tylers where Rosalie Hoag was living.

Polly's court date for the murder of her daughter Frances was set for March 17th. In the meantime Dr. Cotes made periodic checkups on Polly, visiting her once or twice a month, including pulling a bad tooth on the 13th of March. She was deemed well and fit to stand trial. Stanley Filkins was prepared as well. He assisted with this case eighteen days in the month of February and fourteen days in March.

A report of the prisoners in the jail was taken in March, just as every other time before one of Polly's trials. Aside from the usual burglary, assault, and larceny cases, Polly was not alone in her crime. A man by the name of David Curry was being held on a charge of murder.

The trial began on Thursday, March 17, 1859. This time Alvin Pease and Hiram W. Hascall took turns bringing Polly Frisch to court. The trial would be as long and as grueling as was the trial for the murder of Henry. Not only would they hold sessions in the morning and afternoon, but some evenings as well. It would last five days. Shortly after noon, the prisoner was brought in to take her seat beside her counsel. As in the other trials, Polly was accompanied by her father, Schubel Franklin.

It became difficult to find men to serve on the jury. Many had already been eliminated during the first two trials. Once again the panel was exhausted, and alternate talismen were subpoenaed by Sheriff Pease. Finally, a jury of twelve was assembled together with the Honorable Judge Noah Davis Jr. presiding. As before, the law firm of Wakeman & Bryan defended Polly Frisch. To assist them, M.F. Robertson was enlisted. George Bowen led the case for the People, assisted by N.A. Woodward.

It had taken until 3:00 p.m. to find a suitable jury. The following men were chosen. William W. Vallett (Foreman), Thomas Bump, Hiram P. Flanders, William Waterman, James Shepard, Silias Cathcart, Orlando Earll, Frederick Fidler, Charles Bonesteel, Charles W. Rumsey, John W. Woodruff, and Nathan E. Hollister.

The Republican Advocate, March 22nd, described Polly Frisch's demur in the following manner:

> She looked careworn, more so than on her previous trials, and evidently felt deeply the awful situation in which she is placed. She possesses a most impassive countenance: is a woman of great self-control and determination, or she would have been completely worn out by the two public trials she has already undergone, to say nothing of the long time she has passed in prison awaiting her trials.

Impassive was a good word to describe Polly Frisch. She sat next to her counsel showing no emotion as N.A. Woodward began his opening speech for the prosecution. Woodward faced the jury as he spoke. He informed them that he expected to prove that the prisoner had spoken often of her desire to get rid of her children. He told the jury about Polly telling others that she could get along just fine without them around and of the fortuneteller's prophecy that they would not live long. He went on to explain that he intended to show that Frances was at a neighbor's house the day before her death and was perfectly healthy. When Frances suddenly took ill the next day, Polly refused to get a physician for the child and she died. Woodward finished by saying that Polly Frisch had purchased arsenic and that arsenic was found in the stomach of the child. With the opening argument finished, the People called their first witness, Robert Almay, to the stand.

The prosecution started this trial in the same manner as the one for Henry's death. They began their line of questioning with the exhumation of Frances' body. As in Henry's trial, Almay related his experience on the day he was present when Frances' remains were dug up. In turn, Reuben Warren, Stanley Filkins, Robert Baker, and Dr. Oliver P. Clark all testified to their involvement in securing the portion of the stomach of the child Frances. In following the pattern of the first trial, the defense tried to dispute each witness's testimony on cross examination as to whether the contents of the seed box were secure or could have been tampered with.

To close the morning session, District Attorney George Bowen called Professor George Hadley to the stand. Once again he stated his experience and professional standing to show he was qualified in the field of chemical toxicology. Professor Hadley elaborated on his analysis of the stomach of Frances Hoag. When asked about his findings, the professor left no doubts in the jury's mind. Hadley testified that upon chemical analysis and various experiments the results were conclusive. There was no doubt that there was a large quantity of arsenic in the stomach. He also matter-of-factly stated that based on the results of his testing, no substance could have been dropped into the contents of the stomach after it had been removed.

There was no disputing the findings this time, nor any other accidents to take in to consideration. The only way that the arsenic could have entered the body of Frances Hoag was if someone had given it to her on something she ingested. The question was how? If the jury was taken aback by this testimony, the evening session would cause even more drama. Not only would Albert Hoag take the stand against his mother, so would his sister Rosalie.

The trial adjourned for the morning. There was no court during the afternoon on this day in the case of the People vs. Polly Frisch. The jurors and the spectators filed back in the courtroom at approximately four o'clock to begin the evening session. While Hadley's testimony of the presence of arsenic was still fresh in the jury's mind, Bowen called the children of Polly Frisch to the stand.

Albert Hoag was sworn in and briefly told about himself. He was now thirteen and still living in Michigan with his Uncle Lyman Hoag. He stated to the court that the defendant was his mother. With the basics out of the way, Bowen got right to the point. Albert was asked to tell the court about the day that Frances took ill and died.

"Mother gave Rosalie and Frances some bread and butter, not a very small piece. Frances ate hers all up. Rosalie ate a part of hers and laid the rest on the table. Frances ate that afterwards. Pretty soon after that, they were both sick, they puked. Frances died the next day. Rosalie was sick in the same way," responded Albert.

On cross-examination Albert did not sway from his story. Albert testified, "Mother did not give me any bread and butter, never gave me any bread and butter that I know of. They were sick a few minutes. Frances cramped and puked. She was not sick until after she ate the other piece of bread and butter."

It was a lucky thing for Rosalie that she did not finish her piece of bread and butter. Unfortunately for Frances, she not only ate her whole piece, but also the rest of her sister's. Frances had taken an overdose of arsenic. Polly had told Mrs. Bateman that she was going to mix the arsenic with bread and butter to kill the rats. Instead, she used it to try to kill her children.

Maybe Polly had hoped that it would be perceived as an accident. If questioned, she could always say that the children had got into it by themselves. That would have worked, had Polly not prepared the bread and butter herself. She could have never predicted that the incident would go this far. After all, it had worked on Henry and no one suspected anything at the time. Why not try it again on her daughters? We still contend that the poisoning was not done to Albert because he served a purpose. Someone was needed to do the chores, at least for a while.

The courtroom was once again dumbstruck when ten-year-old Rosalie Hoag took the stand to testify against her mother. Rosalie began by saying she had been living in Chautauqua County for a little over two years with an uncle, but at the time of Frances' death, she was living with her mother in Alabama. In a touching moment Rosalie commented that she had been down after tea to see her mother before court reconvened.

One can only imagine the emotional turmoil for Rosalie at this meeting. She was such a young girl to be visiting her mother in a jail cell because her mother had murdered her father and sister. It must have crossed her mind, that in a few short hours, she would take the witness stand to tell a room full of people how her mother did it—how her mother tried to poison her as well. It is hard to envision the two together and what they would have said to each other. Did Polly say, "I love you," or, "Please Rosalie, you don't want mommy to hang, do you?"

Whatever they discussed, Rosalie took the stand that evening and was sworn in. "Am ten years old; should be put in jail if I did not tell the truth."

Rosalie began her testimony, "Franky was younger than I. I remember her dying. I was sick too. Before Franky died, mother went up to the Corners, went with horse and wagon. I was at Mrs. Bugby's while she was gone. Mother gave us some bread and butter after we got home. Albert was not there when she gave it to us. He was outdoors. She ate hers and I ate part of mine. Franky took what I had left and ate it; we were well the rest of the day; she was not taken sick till the next day. When taken sick she was paring potatoes; she puked and I did; I was not sick the same time that she was. Frances died the day after she was taken sick."

On cross-examination the defense angled at the possibility of Rosalie being fed the answers. Rosalie responded, "My Uncle's folks came here with me. No one talked with me before I came. Me and Albert talked about the bread and butter. I talked about it first; then Albert. We did not quite agree. This was the day before yesterday."

Rosalie implied that her uncle's family did not direct her in what to say, nor did Albert, as she states they did not quite agree. The disagreement was not over the bread and butter itself, but which day they got sick. Rosalie thought it was not until the following day (Monday) and that Frances died the day after that (Tuesday). We know by Frances' death date, other testimony, and court papers that Frances died on Monday the 11th of August not Tuesday the 12th. We must bear in mind that the girl was only seven at the time of the murders. She remembered the important part well enough. Her mother had given them bread and butter. Frances, who ate a portion and a half, had died. This time it was not Albert's testimony alone relaying what their mother had done. Rosalie, a victim herself, had verified the act.

The final witness for the evening session of the first day was James McComb. James testified he was at the house the day before Frances died, and that no physician had been called for the child. The child vomited while he was there, which he described as, "green then yellow, then like the slobber of a horse." Frances' vomiting might have been the only thing that kept her alive for a few hours longer. The usual question was asked by the defense when it was their turn to question the witness. James was asked if he saw Polly mistreat her children.

James replied, "I did not discover any unkindness towards her children, on her part."

The first day of the trial covered some very enlightening witnesses. Judge Noah Davis adjourned court to reconvene the next morning. The 18th would be a long day. Deputy Olcott was busy traveling to bring in two witnesses—Betsy Lester and Mrs. Barber. Based on his mileage it appears that they were no longer living in the vicinity of the town of Alabama.

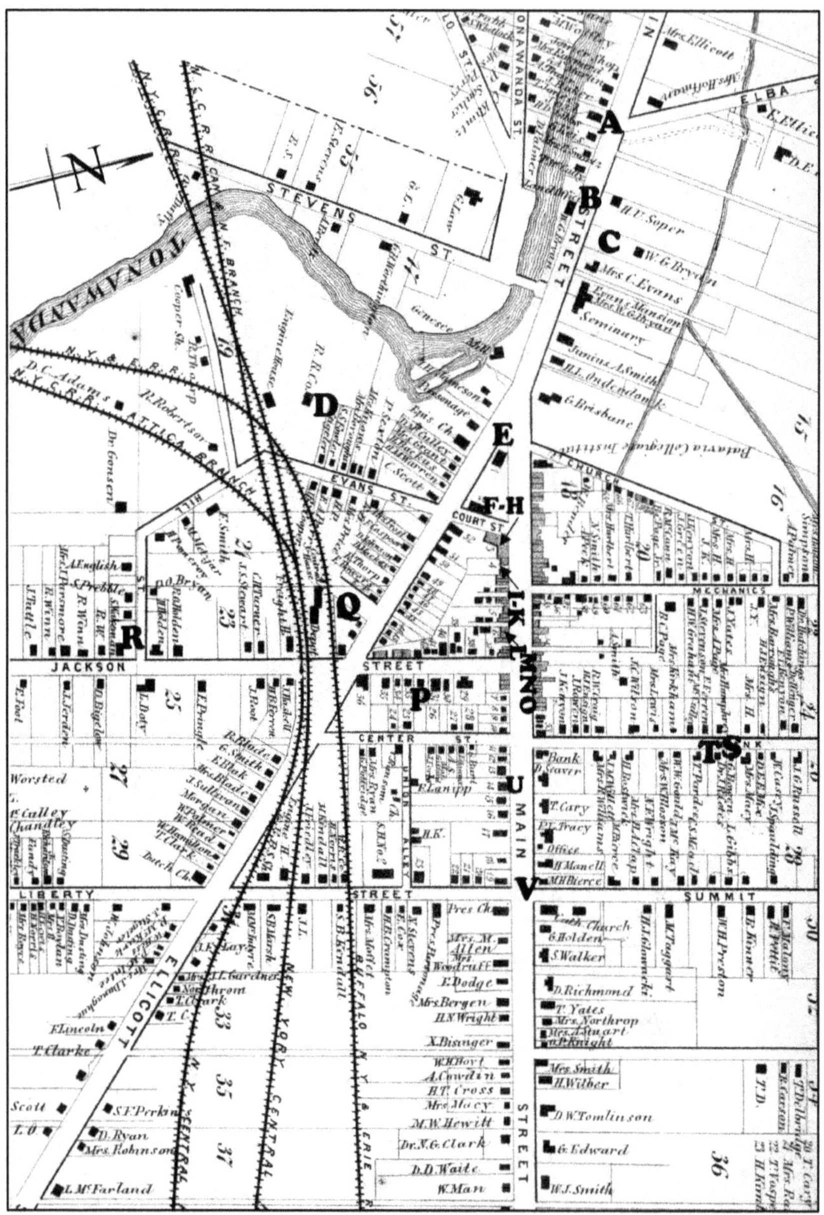

Figure 15. Village of Batavia (Now City of Batavia)

Composite Map - mid-1850s

Batavia Locations

A - OLD JAIL - South side of Main Street.
B - HOLLAND LAND OFFICE - South side of Main Street. The Holland Land Office is now the Museum of Genesee County under the direction of the Holland Purchase Historical Society.
C - WILLIAM BRYAN RESIDENCE - North side of Main St.
D - ALVIN PEASE RESIDENCE - West side of Evans Street.
E - OLD COUNTY COURT HOUSE - Corner of Main Street and Court Street.
F - EAGLE BLOCK - Eagle Hotel - Corner of Main Street and Court Street.
G - GEORGE BOWEN LAW OFFICE (above Post Office) - South side of Main Street. West of the Eagle Hotel.
H - N.A. WOODWARD LAW OFFICE - South side of Main Street. West of Bowen's Law Office.
I - BROWN & GLOWACKI LAW OFFICE - South side of Main Street.
J - OLIVER P. CLARK DRUGGIST and THE REPUBLICAN ADVOCATE NEWSPAPER - South side of Main Street.
K - WAKEMAN & BRYAN LAW OFFICE - South side of Main St.
L - THE WESTERN HOTEL - South side on Main Street.
M - BATAVIA DEMOCRAT NEWSPAPER - North side of Main St.
N - SPIRIT OF THE TIMES NEWSPAPER - North side of Main Street.
O - DR. HOLTON GANSON'S OFFICE - North side of Main Street.
P - DR. ROBERT BAKER'S OFFICE - West side of Center Street.
Q - TRAIN DEPOT - Near Jackson Street and Ellicott Street.
R - SETH WAKEMAN RESIDENCE - Corner of Jackson & Hill Streets.
S - GEORGE BOWEN RESIDENCE - East side of Bank Street.
T - DR. JOHN COTES RESIDENCE - East side of Bank Street. Directly south of Bowen Residence.
U - DR. L.B. COTES OFFICE - South side of Main Street.
V - DR. JOHN B. COTES OFFICE - Corner of Summit Street and Main Street. Father of L.B. Cotes.

Figure 16. Legend for Batavia map in figure 15.

Sessions were held on the Frisch trial in the morning, afternoon, and evening. Once again, almost everyone in the town of Alabama that knew Polly Frisch would testify against her.

At 8:00 a.m. Friday morning the prosecution called the residents of the town of Alabama to the stand one by one. Mrs. McComb spoke of how she asked Polly if the children had eaten green apples and Polly told her they hadn't. Abigail Filkins had also questioned Polly about the apples. Polly had told her they had eaten them and got cholera morbus because of it. That of course could not be possible because that is not how cholera is contracted. Abigail also testified to Polly's plans the day Frances died on Monday the 11th of 1856.

"I was there soon after Frances died," said Abigail. "Polly told me the children were well on Sunday. That she had to go to Batavia on Monday."

After speaking about the green apples, Abigail continued, "I went to see the corpse. Polly did not go in. I removed the cloth from the face and put it in water. It looked purple. I told her it smelt like turpentine. Polly said they had used it on the child. The neck and arms of the child were spotted with purple spots. Lips were dry and parched. I saw blood on the teeth."

Mr. Gumaer testified to the same condition of the corpse when he came to lay out the body of Frances, noticing also froth around the child's mouth.

When cross-examined about Frances' health, the defense questioned Mrs. Filkins, as to whether Frances had sick spells. Abigail answered, "I do not remember that Frances had sick spells." Frances had been the daughter of her nephew Henry. It was obvious she was touched by thoughts of her dead niece when Mrs. Abigail Filkins added, "She was a smart and pretty child."

Abigail also mentioned on re-direct that Polly hadn't sent for Frances' uncle in Chautauqua County on the direction of the doctor. These were Polly's words to Mrs. Filkins, however, and not spoken to Abigail Filkins by the doctor himself. It is more likely that Polly didn't want the relatives in Chautauqua County to know that Frances died so soon after Henry. They must have eventually found out, possibly through Stanley Filkins, as Henry's relations had come to take both Albert and Rosalie away before anything happened to them.

Mrs. Bugby and her daughter, Mrs. Shepard, took the stand next for the prosecution. They insisted that the children were at the Bugby home while Polly had been at Alabama Center. None of the children had gone home early. They stayed until Polly picked them up at 2 p.m. Mrs. Shepard continued with the account of the morning of Frances' death. She spoke of how Polly didn't do anything but give the child sage tea.

Mrs. Shepard testified, "Polly did nothing about getting her a physician. Her mother asked her if she did not want some tea and toast. She said she did not."

Witness after witness told how Polly had repeated the fortune that was told to her about the death of "two of her family." The difference was that Polly changed the wording often to "husband and child" and the version of what they died from changed from person to person as well. Reuben Warren, Lucinda Farley, Eliza Barber and even Julia Maybach testified to the versions they were told of the prediction. Aaron Clark, whose niece it was that told the fortune, testified to the same.

Several Alabama women took the stand to again defame Polly's character. Her feelings toward her husband and children, as we already know, were not a secret in the community. Julia Avery and Eliza Barber minced no words in describing how Polly related to them her desire to be rid of her husband and children. It grew progressively worse for Polly Frisch as each new witness testified.

Eliza Barber also had seen the arsenic wrapped in paper in Polly's bandbox in the fall of 1857. "I asked her what it contained," stated Mrs. Barber to the court. "She said it was arsenic." As to Polly's character Eliza responded, "Have heard prisoner say that she had as lief [gladly] kill her children as rattlesnakes."

The defense, on cross, asked her under what circumstances Polly Frisch had made that statement. Mrs. Barber told the court, "She said this when she was petulant, she seemed excited and out of patience—just as all mothers do when their children have done wrong. When I spoke to her about the arsenic she said her children had known better than to go into her band box."

Once again all the doctors were asked to testify about the exhumation, the appearance of the corpses upon digging them up, and the effects of arsenic poisoning. Dr. Ganson, Dr. Baker, and Dr. Clark were all asked the previous questions. In addition, Dr. Holton Ganson was given a long hypothetical question.

District Attorney Bowen asked, "Suppose a child 6 or 7 years old, perfectly well at 9 o'clock p.m., after eating bread and butter to be taken very sick, vomiting continually, great thirst, cramps in the limbs and stomach; the color of the matter vomited being green and yellow, and these symptoms continued till death which occurs within about 24 hours from the time it was taken, coupled with the fact that immediately after death the corpse frothed about the mouth and was covered with purple spots; also, a liberal quantity of arsenic being found in the stomach by a chemical analysis more than a year after death, what, in your opinion, was the cause of the death?"

Dr. Ganson replied, "I should say that arsenic killed the patient."

Ganson added that the first symptoms of arsenic poison resemble that of cholera morbus, and that spasms and discoloration of the skin would follow.

When District Attorney Bowen asked Dr. Clark the same question he answered, "I would have no doubt but it was arsenic that produced the death. Think no reasonable person could have any doubt."

An unusual witness was called next. She was Mrs. Royce, the wife of the former jail keeper. It seems that she had a conversation in the jail with Polly soon after her arrest.

"My husband formerly kept the jail," began Mrs. Royce. "I had a conversation with the prisoner. I asked her if she had not had arsenic in the house and given it by mistake. She said she had not, she never had any in the house - did not know the color of it."

When cross-examined as to when this conversation took place she answered, "This was when the examination was progressing soon after she was arrested."

Although Polly adamantly defended her innocence and said she did not have any arsenic in the house, and did not even know what it looked like, it showed Polly Frisch to be a liar. The Bateman's once again testified how Polly had bought the arsenic on two separate occasions. Polly bought it from two different people, others had seen it in her box, and her own sister said she had bought it. Professor Hadley had also tested the box that the arsenic was kept in and it tested positive. All were points for the prosecution and not the defense. With this, the prosecution rested its case. The following excerpt is taken from the *Republican Advocate* newspaper:

> The opening for the defense was made by W.G. Bryan, Esq., in a masterly manner. We have seldom, if ever, heard a more powerful plea. He examined the evidence introduced by the prosecution in every able manner, in a speech, which occupied nearly an hour, and then stated concisely what the defense expected to prove. The speech was listened to in breathless attention by a crowded auditory, and, let the case terminate as it may, the prisoner can have no reason to doubt that her counsel have done all for her which could be done.

The hour was getting late. Only two witnesses would be called to the stand this day for the defense, Schubel Franklin and Julia Maybach. Schubel was called to testify first. In a very lengthy testimony, Polly's father gave a full account of his version of what had happened during the twenty-four hours that lead up to Frances' death. In his testimony, Schubel conveniently forgot several incidents. That, or he wasn't very interested in what had happened that day to Frances and Rosalie because he was focused on the fire in the woods. Still, he didn't even recall Rosalie being sick.

"I went to the front door and looked and saw Frances coming from towards the barn. She ran up to her mother and said 'Mother, I'm sick'. Pretty quick she began to vomit."

Schubel testified how he had yelled at Polly about the girl eating green fruit. Schubel continued, "I could not say whether she laid her on the lounge before I spoke. Noble soon came in. I think she vomited while we were at dinner. Don't recollect her vomiting more before dinner. When we had dinner Rosalie sat down to eat. I got up. Franky was not on the lounge. I don't know where Rosalie slept that night, she was not sick to my knowledge."

Schubel was of course asked about Polly's care of the children. Her father answered, "Franky and Rosalie once in a while had sick spells. Franky was the flower of the family. I never saw Polly unkind to the children. She was always kind to them when sick. Hoag left a little homestead to Polly and the children. Polly had the children taken from the old burying ground and put into new. She bought a lot, and put up stones for all the family."

There are some interesting things about this last bit of Schubel Franklin's testimony. First is the burial ground. There are five cemeteries in Alabama proper that we are aware of. Alabama Center Cemetery is where the Hoag's are buried now. The one that was called the "burial ground" we now call the Basom Plot. We discovered a separate deed for this cemetery, with its first burial in 1838, calling it the "Burying Ground of School District #8." All the stones are now gone from this plot. We are not sure who is buried there, other than those accounted for in the book, *Tombstone Inscriptions From the*

Abandoned Cemeteries and Farm Burials of Genesee County by LaVerne C. Cooley.

The reason this is important is that there is no stone for Eliza Jane Hoag or the mysterious infant born subsequent to Henry's death at the Hoag plot in the Alabama Center Cemetery. The bodies must have been moved prior to the inquests as records show the exhumations were performed at the cemetery in Alabama Center. There is however a space between the grave of Henry and those of his children.

Figure 17. Hoag family plot, Alabama Center Cemetery. From left to right: Henry, (space), Frances, Roselphe & Leonard, Viola.

Photo by C. Amrhein.

So the question remains—are Eliza Jane and the infant buried with no headstone? At least Eliza Jane should be, and maybe her stone has been destroyed with time. The original cemetery records burned in a fire in the early 1900s and had to be recreated from the tombstones themselves. If Eliza Jane's stone had been destroyed by that point in time there would be no record of her burial there.

What of the infant that was born after Henry died, the child that was allegedly Matthew Bardwell's? Would Polly have buried that child with the rest of the Hoag children and continue the charade or would she have left it in the old burial ground? It would be fascinating to know who was buried in the unknown grave, if anyone. Unless, when Polly had the family moved she reserved a space for herself. It turns out that this may be the case. In looking at the photograph of the plot, there is room for an adult between Henry and Frances. Eliza Jane and the infant might be buried together, as were siblings Leonard and Roselphe. We came across some new information since our first publishing in a rather unexpected source—a book titled *Christ and the Gallows: Or, Reasons for the Abolition of Capital Punishment.*

In the mid-1860s, Marvin Henry Bovee, the author, conducted a canvass throughout the state of New York on behalf of those against capital punishment. One of the men opposed to the practice was none other than, William G. Bryan, Polly's attorney. In his letter addressed to Mr. Bovee, dated November 12, 1865, he wrote about two cases—that of David Curry (in jail for murder the same time Polly was in 1859) and Polly Frisch. In the letter, reprinted in the above mentioned book, William Bryan wrote the following concerning the timeframe before the trials commenced:

> She had the bodies of her husband and children removed from the old grave-yard to the new cemetery, paid for

> the new lot herself, bought tombstones, which she paid for in sewing, and left a little space between Hoag's and little Frankie's graves, where she was to be buried. She never attempted to escape and always denied her guilt. When the accusations against her first became current, she called at our office and insisted upon having a slander suit brought against certain parties; and requested that the bodies be disinterred and analyzed. From careful inquiry, we were satisfied that, on the evidence treating her as sane, she could not be convicted; for there seemed to be an utter want of sane motive for the commission of the triple murder.

From records we know it was not the defense's side that requested the exhumation of the Hoags. By the time the case proceeded to other trials, however, Bryan would change his opinion on Polly's sanity.

The other interesting point about Schubel Franklin's testimony was his remark that Henry had left a little homestead for Polly and the children. That just wasn't true, and Schubel himself knew it wasn't true. Henry Hoag died without a will. He left nothing to anyone. It was the court that decided who inherited the property and it wasn't Polly. It was given to the children, in trust. Unless of course they died, then Polly would be the rightful owner. We believe Schubel said Henry left a homestead to Polly and the children to make it seem that they were a loving family, that Henry left his home to his devoted wife and children.

Schubel Franklin's testimony took up a good deal of the court's time. He was no doubt exhausted as he left the witness box. His daughter Julia was to take the stand next to give her rendition of the death of Frances Hoag.

After Julia's long statement she pointed out, "I did not see any spots until after I commenced rubbing [with the turpentine and camphor]. Franky had sick spells before."

Only Schubel and Julia refer to the children having sick spells. Still, sick spells are different than being in the throes of an agonizing death.

Julia continued by saying, "I never saw any want of affection on the part of the defendant towards her children. I drank the remainder of the sage tea."

The last remark seems to be overkill on Julia's part. Both her father and Julia were desperately trying to save Polly from the gallows. Why would she drink the rest of the tea? What would be the point of saying that she had? We are of the opinion that Julia only said that to try and show that the tea wasn't poisoned. If they truly believed that Frances was sick with cholera, no one in their right mind would have drank the tea knowing how contagious and deadly the disease was.

It was now the turn of the prosecution to cross-examine the witness. Julia had testified before Judge Cowdin during Polly's arraignment as to the paper that contained the arsenic. She testified to seeing it and to what size it was. When George Bowen asked her about it she replied, "I do not recollect testifying before Cowdin that the paper in which the arsenic was purchased was 4 inches square."

This did not seem of much importance at the time, but it would the next day when Judge Cowdin would be called to the stand on re-direct by the prosecution. Julia had changed her version as to what size of paper the arsenic was put in. The defense was finished with Julia and with their witnesses for the day. Court was adjourned until the following morning. Julia had put herself in an awful position in her attempt to save the sister she was so close to. Her testimony had been fairly long and had taxed her strength. The stress and high emotions would soon wear her down and cause her physical complications. Julia may not have known it yet, but she was pregnant with her second child.

On Saturday morning, March 19th, court reconvened with the defense ready to call its last witnesses to the stand. Eliza Franklin and Charles Noble, as well as his wife, all testified to Polly's diligent care of the children. Once again, these were Polly's relatives defending her. Mrs. Lorenzo Clark and Mrs. Aaron Clark appeared as character witnesses to state how kind and affectionate Polly was. The only chance the defense had was to show the jury that all the horrible things that the prosecution's witnesses had said about Polly were untrue.

George Bowen cross-examined Polly's mother. It was too hard to believe that these people never saw Polly lose her temper with her youngsters.

"I saw freaks of passion in her, same as other mothers. She sometimes humored the children, and then got out of patience with them," said Eliza Franklin.

Wakeman and Bryan, with no other witnesses to call, rested their case. George Bowen took the floor again and recalled several witnesses to the stand: Mrs. Shepard, Mrs. Betsy Lester, and Selah Vosburg. The point of this was to get the last impression in the minds of the jury and to stress that the children were at Mrs. Bugby's home the entire day until Polly returned for them. He wanted to eliminate any thoughts that the children were left unsupervised. Selah Vosburg added that the day he went to appraise the property after Henry died Polly had been harsh towards her children.

Augustus Cowdin, the judge during Polly's arraignment, was the last person called to enter the witness box. We thought it to be quite unusual for a judge to take the stand to speak about a previous case tried in his own court. Judge Cowdin told the jury that Julia had described the size of the paper containing the arsenic differently during the trial he presided over. Julia had changed her testimony during this trial for some reason. It might have been to imply that there wasn't a large amount of arsenic wrapped in the paper, not as much as Professor Hadley had indicated was in the remains of Frances. Julia's testimony could be viewed in many ways. One, that Polly had only a little to begin with and not enough to kill anybody; or two, that there wasn't much left because Polly had already used it on her family. Her change in description could also mean she never saw it in the first place. It would all depend on how the jury interpreted it.

No further witnesses were called on either side after Augustus Cowdin testified. Seth Wakeman addressed the jury on behalf of his client for three hours with "great ability and force" printed the *Republican Advocate*. The *Republican Advocate*, in their March 22nd issue had the following to say about the prosecution:

> Mr. Bowen, Dist. Attorney, closed on the part of the People. His summing up was quite lengthy; reviewing all the

> testimony very ably, after which, Judge Davis delivered his charge to the Jury. This was the most able effort of the kind which we have ever heard from the Bench. It was done in great fairness and impartiality, neither seeking to obtain from any Jury member upon him as a Judge, nor accepting to interfere with the rights of the Jury. At about 1/2 past 5 in the evening the Jury retired to deliberate.

The jury was taken to the Eagle Tavern, a short distance away from the court house, for the length of the deliberations. From the start the jury had problems agreeing on the guilt or innocence of Polly Frisch, and debated the issue all through Sunday. The jury was sequestered until they returned at eight o'clock Monday morning of the 21st. The courtroom was packed and impatiently waiting for the decision of the jurors. The result was recounted in the various local newspapers:

> The Court then put the usual question as to whether they agreed on the verdict.
>
> Wm. W. Vallett, Esq., their foreman, rose and said, "No, we have not."
>
> Judge Davis then asked him, "If given more time, would you be able to reach a decision?"
>
> Mr. Vallett replied, "There is no prospect of agreement. We are equally divided and have stood so for 24 hours. There has been no change among us. We have stood six against six from the first."

Judge Noah Davis thanked the jury for their serious attention to the matter and discharged them from any further duty. It was a hung jury. The case would have to be tried again. In the March 24th Issue of the *Buffalo Daily Courier* the newspaper reported their view:

> It is certainly a very remarkable case —one that demands the greatest care, patience and humanity in its investigation, and one which no outside clamor or prejudice should be allowed to operate unfairly against the prisoner. It is credited to Genesee county that so little trouble has been found in selecting juries in these repeated trials; and it is hoped that the last trial will be conducted with the same humanity that have characterized its predecessors. The reputation of the eminent Judge (Marvin,) who holds the next Genesee Circuit, is a guarantee that while justice will be duly administrated, the rights of the prisoner—however humble and defenseless she may be—will not be disregarded.

Being from outside the community, they were not aware of the goings-on behind the scenes and how many men had been gone through in order to find an impartial jury. Polly Frisch was described as a poor, defenseless, innocent victim in the whole affair. The *LeRoy Gazette*, a hometown newspaper, described her much differently in their report that hit the newsstands on the 23rd of March:

> This wretched woman has just undergone a third trial, at Batavia, for the murder of a third member of her family by administering poison. ... The evidence of her guilt seems almost incontrovertible, yet the jury failed to convict. ... The plan of taking men who do not read newspapers, and consequently "are not prejudiced," is simply ridiculous. This is the rule, but we do not know that the jury who tried this case were selected for their abstemiousness in this particular.— *One* of the jurors at least takes and reads a newspaper, and we presume they all do.

As had happened so many times before, Polly Frisch was returned to the jail cell that had become her home. In retrospect, the jurors were getting closer and closer to the verdict of guilty. Naturally, everyone in the county was reading the account of the trial that was printed in the *Republican Advocate*, and Polly's lawyers knew it. The prosecution knew it. The team of Wakeman & Bryan had a gut feeling that they would not be so lucky the next time they brought their client Polly Frisch into court.

17

FRANCES – Trial No. 2

One person can carry a heavy load for only so long before it becomes impossible to bear. Obviously Polly didn't want to be convicted of murder, but the uncertainty of not knowing surely would have been too much for her. She had been alone, day after day for almost two years, the only female prisoner in the jail. Imagine the anxiety that built up before each court appearance. During each trial she sat for hours on end in the courtroom, spectators staring, listening to all her neighbors repeat over and over events she wished she could forget or wished had never happened. It was too late now for regrets; she just wanted it to be over.

We now start to see a connection between the court dates and the medical treatment administered by Dr. John Cotes. Not before a trial, but always afterwards. We at first theorized that the treatment was stress related. The March trial had been grueling, and soon she would have to do it all over again for the fourth time. It would be emotionally overwhelming. Dr. Cotes visited Polly ten times in the month of April, twice during the night on the 9th. One would have to wonder if these were periodic mental breakdowns. The episode passed, but Dr. Cotes made a routine visit on the 2nd and 27th of May, and once again on June 9th. It appeared for the moment that Polly Frisch was in stable condition.

The trial was not postponed this time due to illness. The prosecution continued on schedule with a court date set for June 30th. Stanley Filkins was once again involved in organizing the statements that had been taken from prospective witnesses. On June 28th, twenty-three men were summoned and sworn in for the various grand jury cases that were scheduled to be held during the June term of the Oyer & Terminer. On a motion by district attorney George Bowen, and granted by the court, fifty extra talismen were called for the Frisch case alone. Based on past experience, Bowen knew that the men who were already called wouldn't be nearly enough.

The usual witnesses were subpoenaed to appear in court for the People. Albert came from Michigan again with his Uncle Lyman, and the Tylers brought Rosalie. As before, others were on the witness list that we have no testimony for. We have no way of knowing if they ever testified, but they were called into court. They were Ellen and Della Losee, ___ Morse, ___ Rapp and wife, ___ Glen, ___ Ralph, ___ Bunce, ___ Prise, E. Lacey, and ___ Flanders. We know their last names because they are taken from county records. The witnesses for the defense, we assume, were part of the files of the law firm of Wakeman & Bryan. Unfortunately, we were unable to locate any records locally or through the State or National Archives on who Polly's defense lawyers called to testify.

The inconvenience these repeated trials caused the entire town of Alabama was taken into consideration this time. Due to financial hardship, several of the witnesses were paid to drop everything to attend the trial. We must remember the lifestyle of the era in which this was taking place. This was the fourth trial, and the fourth time dozens of people in one town were being pulled away from their lives.

The majority of the witnesses were men. They were the financial providers for their families. Businessmen, including the town doctors, were to be stuck in Batavia again for days at a time. Farms were not being tended to properly. The last trial had interfered with working up the fields to prepare for planting season. Then there were the daily duties that were involved in caring for the livestock, feeding, milking, and stable and barn chores. This was a very bad year for farmers. An insect known as the wheat midge was devastating the wheat crops. There were problems with their other crops as well. There had been two bad frosts already—one in May and another at the beginning of June. None of the crops were growing as they should be, including the fruit trees.

With many of Alabama's residents in Batavia attending the trials, who was running the town, tending the fields, the stores, the post office, or the doctor's offices? Now the county wanted them all back at the end of the month, when farmers were in the process of cultivating their corn and trying desperately to salvage their crops. The doctors were busy treating summer illnesses, and people needed the general stores open to purchase supplies that the duties of summer brought. The county had no choice but to compensate the witnesses for the income they would lose.

Like a reoccurring nightmare, Polly Frisch was escorted into court on June 30, 1859 by Sheriff Alvin Pease. The trial would last seven days, ending on July 6th, and would be the longest of all the trials to date. It wasn't just Genesee County anymore that wanted this woman to be convicted. This time James C. Smith, Esq. of Canandaigua, conducted the case for the prosecution, assisted by George Bowen.

Smith was the assistant attorney general for the State of New York. He was to handle the case under the direction of Attorney General Lyman Tremain, and at the expense of the State. One has to wonder if the state stepped in due to the several mishaps in trying to get this murder case cleared on a local level.

John H. Martindale, Esq., of Rochester would help Seth Wakeman and William Bryan conduct the case for the defense. Judge Benjamin F. Greene would preside over the courtroom. Witnesses who were brought in from out of town were lodged at the Western Hotel; the jurymen were put up at the Eagle Hotel. Both were on Main Street in Batavia and fairly close to each other as well as to the Court House.

We found no record of testimony for this trial. The newspapers covered the story, but there was no account of the proceedings. Only the verdict was published. There really was no point in covering the specifics this time around. The same witnesses were called for this trial as the last, and they no doubt gave basically the same testimony. It had all been said before. The only thing the public was interested in now was if the jury would finally find her guilty.

As expected, most of the men who were picked for the grand jury to serve on the Frisch case were eliminated. It was not expected, however, to go through the fifty talismen as well. Forty more were summoned for jury duty and it still was not enough. Ultimately, 114 men had to be called into court before they found twelve, who hopefully, were unbiased enough to serve as jurors.

Despite the repeat of the witnesses and their testimony, this trial would be much different than the last three had been. It was not the trial itself, but what happened behind the scenes while the trial was in progress, and after it was over, that is of interest.

District Attorney George Bowen was tired of trying this woman on the same crime without getting a conviction. He was positive that Polly Frisch was a murderess. The chemical analysis that had been done on Frances was now a year and a half old. What if he had Professor George Hadley perform the testing again? If arsenic was still detected after almost two years, there could be no dispute that a large amount of the poison had been given at the time of Frances' death. As horrible as it may seem, the body of Frances Hoag was once again raised from the grave.

Since there was no detailed coverage of this trial we have no way of knowing who was present at the time of this exhumation, or the chain of events surrounding the event. It was only found through piecing two small elements of documentation together, that in themselves had made no sense. Because of a bill presented to the county by the carriage driver who drove the officials around to perform their duties, and a bill attached to a letter from Professor George Hadley, we knew that the remains of Frances had been exhumed again. Also, some affidavits came to light in this case and when put together with the previous mentioned documents, painted a very clear picture of what transpired during this trial.

It was Saturday, July 2nd, and the case was in progress in Batavia. In the meantime, Frank Scripter, the carriage driver for the county, was instructed by the court to take the doctors once again to Alabama. The doctors' names aren't mentioned in the bill. The purpose was to get a fresh portion of the stomach of Frances Hoag for the Frisch case.

Professor George Hadley had attended the trial every day. He was to be called to the stand to testify again but he just wasn't sure when. The hour was getting late so he knew he would not be taking the stand on the 2nd. When court adjourned for the day, Hadley went back to his room at the Western Hotel.

Figure 18. Western Hotel, building on far right. Main Street, Batavia, NY. (No longer standing.)

Photo courtesy of the Genesee County History Department.

A little before midnight, on that same Saturday night, George Hadley was paid a visit. He was instructed to get on the train for Buffalo and head back to his lab. He was to do further analysis and report back at nine o'clock on Monday morning. He was then handed a new box containing a recently obtained portion of the stomach of Frances Hoag. This must have been very tight timing since the last train going west, was on the Buffalo New York & Erie Railroad, and it was to leave at 12:15 a.m. It was the only train out that late at night. Hadley obliged the request and left for Buffalo.

George Hadley and one of his assistants conducted a new series of tests all day that Sunday and into the night. If it wasn't for his assistant's help, Hadley said it would have been beyond his hope of accomplishing in so short of time. The test was once again conclusive and without any doubt. With the analysis finished, the professor prepared to leave from Buffalo for the Genesee County Court House. He hadn't gotten much rest over the weekend with most of his time being devoted to the work.

The only train leaving Buffalo to get Hadley to Batavia in time was the New York Central Railroad. Professor Hadley must have caught the 8 a.m. train out of Buffalo, which arrived in Batavia at approximately 9:04 a.m. on Monday the 4th of July. He immediately reported his findings to the district attorney. (Although 4th of July was celebrated it was not yet a Federal holiday. Court was held the same as any other weekday.) Before noon that day, the professor gave his testimony to the findings of a large amount of arsenic in the remains of Frances Hoag. After almost two years it was still detectable.

Aside from the evidence given by the other witnesses, including Albert and Rosalie, Hadley's findings must have weighed heavy in the jury's minds. Little did the prosecution know that the yet unknown events of the last few days would destroy their case.

The trial continued into the next day. Polly appeared in the courtroom smiling and talking to those who came to greet her. She was sure in her mind, as many others were, that the jury would not agree. If this happened again, it would be over, and Polly Frisch would be freed. Finally, on Tuesday afternoon of the 5th, the jury retired to deliberate the prisoner's fate.

The jury was out for almost twenty-four hours before reaching a decision. On Wednesday, July 6, 1859 at 11:00 a.m., the jurors filed back into court and entered the jury box. Polly was lead into the courtroom, like so many times before, by Sheriff Alvin Pease. She was in a cheerful mood as she stepped with confidence to take her place by her counsel. The crowd was on the edge of their seats as they awaited the verdict. Had they agreed this time? Polly was sure that they had not, and was probably already planning her first day of freedom.

The room was hushed as the court clerk stood and asked the foreman, James L. Pierson, if they had agreed upon a verdict.

"We have," the foreman answered.

The prisoner was told to face the jury, and the jury the prisoner.

Pierson was then asked, "How do you find? Guilty or not guilty?"

"Guilty," he replied.

By newspaper accounts, Polly was in shock. She didn't move a muscle. She couldn't believe what she was hearing. Polly didn't break down until the jury was polled one by one. Each man answered individually, in a clear voice for all to hear, "Guilty." Not until then did she break down into tears.

Judge Greene immediately sentenced the prisoner. Polly Frisch was found guilty of murder in the first degree for the death of her daughter Frances Hoag. She was to return to court on Saturday the 9th for sentencing. Polly no doubt thought it was over. She was going to hang. She needed no direction from Sheriff Pease as she was taken back to the county jail.

The jurors, with the case now over, began to discuss the events of the last few days with reporters and spectators. Rumors began circulating throughout the courtroom. One of the jurors mentioned in conversation that Henry M. Coon, who also had sat on the jury, had looked at the Judge's notes in the Minute Book on the proceedings of the trial. That this had happened before the jury had reached their verdict. Someone else made the remark, "Wasn't that one of the jurymen we saw out together on Sunday?" Still another spectator was sure it was one of the jurors he saw sitting in the lobby of the Eagle Hotel, with no supervision, reading a newspaper. Conversation continued as people slowly left the building on their journeys towards home.

By the following afternoon, Thursday the 7th, Seth Wakeman and William Bryan had caught wind of what had happened. They quickly prepared a motion to the court to declare a mistrial.

If it weren't for the irresponsibility of the jury and the constables to their duties, Polly would have been on her way to the hangman's noose. This was a miracle for the defense, an unbelievable stroke of luck. It was pretty clear, even to the prosecution, that Polly Frisch did not get a fair trial. If the court granted the motion presented by the defense, District Attorney Bowen would have no choice but to try the case again. The prosecution had to prepare to do what they could to argue against the request that the defense presented to the judge.

For the next two days, and on Monday and Tuesday the following week, the twelve jurors were subpoenaed back into court. For four days Frank Scripter, the carriage driver, drove one of the constables to pick up the jurymen to question them on their conduct while they were supposed to be sequestered. Signed and notarized affidavits were taken from each man. All attested to the fact that they spoke to no one, but it wasn't true. The truth would soon come out, as one by one, residents would come forward to write out sworn affidavits stating they saw the jury meandering about Batavia.

As with all the other documentation we have found on the case of Polly Frisch, we pieced together chronologically the events of July 3rd through the 5th from the numerous affidavits that had been filed. Here is what happened on that Sunday and how the juror gained possession of the Minute Book in the courtroom two days later.

Sunday the 3rd was to be a day of rest, and the jury needed it. It was a difficult task deciding the fate of Polly Frisch. The jurors were lodged at the Eagle Hotel and their rooms were in a separate area from the regular hotel guests. A sitting room had been provided near the hotel lobby for their use only. Under Sheriff Charles Sprague, Deputy Sheriff Lorenzo Olcott, and Constable Robert Pease were in charge of the jury. Their job was to insure that the jury was under constant supervision. They were sequestered, and not to speak to anyone, read anything that may have been in print about the trial, or leave the confines of the Eagle Hotel. All the things the jury was not supposed to do, they did.

On that Sunday morning, Hiram Merill, a local Batavia resident was to meet his friend at the Eagle Hotel. His friend had come from Arkansas for a visit and the two men were to meet that morning for breakfast. Hiram had been following the trial and had attended court on several days. Although Hiram did not know the names of the jurors, he knew them by sight from seeing them in the courtroom.

Figure 19. Eagle Hotel. Batavia, NY. Formerly on the corner of Main and Court Streets.
Photo Courtesy of the Genesee County History Department.

While he was waiting for his friend in the hotel lobby, his attention was called to the public reading room. It was a large room directly opposite to the hotel parlor. There in the room sat two of the jury members, not together with the rest of their group, sitting at a table reading newspapers. Mr. Merill glanced around the rest of the lower floor of the Eagle Hotel to see if his friend had arrived already. He noticed that part of the jury was walking about the large hall and others were milling around in the front parlor that adjoined the hall. All the rooms were in close proximity of each other and well within his view.

While the jury members were sitting at the tables in the reading room, some hotel patrons came in and talked freely about the trial. They were speaking loud enough to each other that the two jurors must have heard them. Hiram heard them conversing, and he wasn't even directly in the room. He saw no officer with or in charge of the jury members, as people continually passed by them while entering and leaving the rooms. This was an active hotel, not just to patrons but the general public.

Hiram Merill, in his affidavit stated, "It is one of the most frequented places of resort in the village of Batavia. The object of the trial was constantly under discussion among the persons sojourning at or standing about the hotel, or sitting in the reading room."

In the meantime two other jurors, James L. Pierson and John Tynell, became bored from sitting all morning doing nothing. They were tired of remaining still for so long without any exercise. The two men got up and left the sitting room. Out the back door of the Eagle Hotel they went, trying not to run into anyone, and into the yard of the hotel. It was nice to get some fresh air, but they still wanted to move around and stretch their legs. The two men walked down the path that led out of the yard, to an alley behind the building, and over to a warehouse that was about fifty-five yards from the hotel. It had seemed to them that they had only been gone ten minutes when they finally returned from their walk and entered the hotel through the side door. They didn't realize so much time had passed since they first left.

James Pierson and John Tynell thought they hadn't been seen, but they had. Merill G. Soper, who lived in the village, noticed them as they strolled by the house of William Seavers' residence on Big Tree Street (now Ellicott) and again a short time later over on Evans Street. He also observed that there was no officer in charge of them.

Around three or four o'clock that same Sunday afternoon, ten of the jurors decided to go out for a short walk around the village. Nathan Bryant and Silas Jones, being tired, had already gone up to their own rooms to take a nap. Charles Sprague remained behind to keep an eye on Bryant and Jones, but remained downstairs in the lobby of the hotel. The other ten jurors, including James Pierson, left the hotel and walked east up Main Street to the cemetery under the supervision of Constable Lorenzo Olcott.

The group passed the home of John Sprague on their outing, which was about a half a mile from the County Court House. John had been to the courthouse during the trial as a spectator and he recognized them as the men of the jury. He noticed that the entire group was not together. He wondered where the other two jurors were.

Silas Jones dozed off as soon as he lay down on his bed. Nathan Bryant, however, had lain there for an hour and still couldn't fall asleep. He rose from his bed and decided to stroll around the hotel a bit thinking maybe that would help. As he was leaving he saw the hotel servant as she passed by his room. Nathan was under no supervision as he went downstairs to the privy that was provided for the jury.

Nathan Bryant was still fidgety, and had no desire to remain still; he had been doing that for days already. He left the sitting room and went down the hall to the other end of the hotel, passing people on his way, and looked out the window there for about twenty minutes. Nathan was restless and this wasn't helping at all. With nothing left to do, he went back upstairs to his room to try and sleep again, but his mind was just too busy to doze off. Nathan heard the call for tea coming from outside his door. Tea might help some, he thought, as he got up and left his room.

Silas Jones was awakened from his sound sleep when he heard that tea was about to be served. As Silas left his room he met up with Nathan Bryant in the hallway. Both men went downstairs into the hotel lobby where Constable Sprague had been waiting. The officer saw the two jurors coming down the stairs and immediately took charge of them.

Silas asked the constable, "Where is the rest of the jury?"

"They got uneasy and walked out a little." Sprague replied.

Nathan Bryant and Silas Jones then went with the constable into the sitting room where they stayed until the rest of the jury returned together with Constable Olcott.

The barkeeper of the Eagle Hotel, George Hall, also noticed that day that the ten jurymen had left the building to freely wander about the village. Hall recalled that the ten men were gone for over three-quarters of an hour before returning. In the meantime, he had seen Nathan Brant roaming the building unattended, and hadn't a clue where Silas Jones had been the entire time.

The jury was technically in the deliberation phase. Even though it was a Sunday, they were supposed to remain together, having no contact with any other persons except for the officers in charge of their supervision. Although Olcott had kept the ten men together on their outing, they should not have been out in the first place. The jury had split, and too many people had seen them do so. Some comments must have been made to the attending officers as they made sure for the remainder of the trial that the jury was kept together. Even though the constables had tightened the reins, their watchful eyes would once again get lazy a couple of days later.

Tuesday, the 5th, had turned out to be a long day for the jurors and lasted into the night. The jury was in the midst of heated deliberations. For hours they had been split on the decision of Polly Frisch's guilt or innocence. Towards morning, the jurymen, with permission from the constable in charge, left the small jury room at the southwest corner of the Court House where they had been sequestered all night. Constable Robert Pease led them down the hallway to stretch their legs and into the main courtroom.

Henry M. Coon, one of the jurors, began meandering around the room, casually glancing at things that were lying about. The others were too busy to notice his movements. They were still intently debating the issues of the case. No one paid any attention to him as he made his way to the front of the courtroom. Lying on the desk in front of Henry Coon was the judge's Minute Book. Curious, Henry opened it. There were quite a lot of notes taken on the trial so far, pages and pages in fact. He came to the notations made by Judge Greene on the testimony of Dr. Cotes. Henry began reading the text quietly out loud. He really wasn't trying to analyze it or even remember it, he was just mindlessly reading to pass the time.

Constable Robert Pease, hearing Henry mumbling to himself, looked around to see where he had gotten. What he saw was not good. The officer quickly made his way to the front of the room, grabbed the book from Henry's hands, and shut it. The constable had no idea that the Minute Book had mistakenly been left in the courtroom. The juror only had the book a moment, but it didn't matter. Coon, as well as the rest of the jury, knew well enough that it was not permitted to refer to any of the documentation at the judge's bench.

The rest of the jurors had seen the commotion, but said nothing. Pease sternly directed Mr. Coon back to the group of his fellow jurors and took them back to the jury room down the hall. Pease knew that if word of this got out, especially after what happened on Sunday, it would surely mean the end of the trial. The constable would see to it that in the future, all of the books would be removed from the courtroom before the jurors were allowed back in.

Up to this point, the jury had been split down the middle just like the last trial. It had seemed at first that the reading of the minutes had gone unnoticed, but it must have come up in their conversations. All of a sudden, everyone was in agreement that Polly Frisch was guilty of murder. After the verdict was read, and the jury discharged the incident was freely discussed amongst them. Those who had been for a verdict of innocent from the beginning were now saying that they had played "possum." They thought she was guilty all along. They only said she was innocent to make sure that the case was debated and that the prisoner got a fair trial. It was a bit unbelievable to have six men be adamantly opposed to a verdict of guilty, then a few moments later change their minds. It was a fortunate thing for Polly that the jurors couldn't resist gabbing about the case the moment it was over.

On Tuesday, less than a week after a verdict of guilty had been reached, the law firm of Wakeman &

Bryan filled a motion with the court to declare a mistrial. The affidavits for both sides were filed in the County Clerk's Office and sent on to Judge Greene for review. The case was argued before him on Thursday the 14th. Upon hearing the evidence, under the circumstances, the judge had no choice but to grant Polly Frisch a new trial. The court date was to be set for sometime in August during a special term of the Oyer & Terminer. Once again, Polly Frisch had been allowed to live just a little bit longer.

18

FRANCES – Trial No. 3

The fifth trial of the People vs. Polly Frisch began on the 25th of August as they commenced interviewing prospective jurors. As usual, they went through the first eighteen men who were called.

> *Genesee County Herald,*
> August 27, 1859
>
> Court of Oyer and Terminer
>
> A special term of this Court convened on Monday, and proceeded to empanel a Jury for a new trial of the case of Polly Frisch, charged with the murder of her child by the administration of arsenic. — It will be remembered that a new trial was granted in the case on the grounds of some irregularity in the proceedings at the last session of this court, when the verdict of guilty was obtained.
>
> Yesterday the testimony of some ten witnesses was gone through with, and it would seem that the case will be again submitted to the jury at an early date.

Fifty more talismen were summoned on the 29th of August, before a panel of twelve men were chosen. As was customary, Polly Frisch was in court during the jury selection process. Polly was visited on the 27th by Dr. Cotes, and administered medicine of some kind. This was the first time she had been medicated during court proceedings. It was necessary for Cotes to tend to Polly on the last two days of July, as well as five days in the month of August. It is only speculation that the drug prescribed was to keep her calm. It would not come out until during this trial that Dr. Cotes had been treating Polly while she was in jail.

Once again, the deputy sheriffs were driven by the carriage driver to pick up witnesses. Lorenzo Olcott was on a longer journey than the rest of the constables. He traveled round trip, for five days, to retrieve Albert and Lyman Hoag from Michigan. Similarly to the previous trials, Rosalie Hoag was escorted by the Tylers. Betsy and George Lester, and the other usual witnesses for the prosecution, were also summoned back into court. District Attorney George Bowen had a surprise witness this time, one of the local doctors who had not been available for the earlier trials.

The prosecution, as expected, enlisted Professor George Hadley into service for the 5th trial. Between the last trial and this one, George Bowen had requested Hadley to come up with a precise amount of arsenic. To state an exact amount would be a bit harder to do. The stomach section he had in his office, although recently taken, had been in the ground over two years. He had already used part of the newest piece for the last trial. Hadley didn't have much left to work with. He still had not been paid for the work he completed in July. Despite that fact, he did what was requested of him, completed the analysis, and testified in court to his positive findings.

When Hadley sent his final bill to the county, he expressed his displeasure over working on this same case with specimens that were in such a decayed condition.

Hadley wrote, "I seldom undertake one of these cases without becoming heartily sick & discouraged many times during its progress—not merely with the tedious & disgusting & unhealthy nature of the work; but also with the anxiety & responsibility attending it. The time alone required to accomplish it properly is not usually less than one month, & I have occasionally been occupied with a single case much longer."

Typically, Professor Hadley was given more time to perform such testing. He had been more than cooperative in assisting Genesee County with their various cases in their attempt to convict Polly Frisch. He should at least have been paid for the work already done. Hadley wasn't the only one who submitted bills to the county more than once without payment. Prosecuting Polly Frisch was costing the county a fortune. They were running out of money.

Schubel Franklin was running out of money, too. It had been a very costly affair to pay for his daughter's defense. Schubel ended up literally "mortgaging the farm" to Seth Wakeman and William Bryan, in order to pay them and John H. Martindale. It would take him until 1866 to pay off the debt.

The trial began on Tuesday, August 30th and would last ten days. It was presided over by Judge Benjamin Greene. Changing strategies, both sides used a fresh approach by having other attorneys take the lead. John H. Martindale Esq. of Rochester, aided by Seth Wakeman and William Bryan, Esqrs., argued the case for the defense. Almost fifty witnesses would be called between both sides. Again, the county paid those with financial hardships for their time to come to Batavia to testify on behalf of the People. Everyone hoped that the jury would reach a verdict this time without any complications.

The trials of Polly Frisch had lost their novelty locally. The courtroom was not as full as it had been when they first began. In fact, it wasn't very crowed at all. What else was left to say? Everyone in the county felt she was guilty. Most of the people from her hometown thought she killed them all. Her own son was sure his mother did it. Even the local reporters weren't covering the trial with their usual vigor. Most of the details were printed in out of town newspapers. The county citizens in general had heard enough. How many times were they going to try this woman before it would end?

The prosecution called its usual witnesses to the stand who testified to the usual things. They were now ready for their surprise witnesses to take the stand. The prosecution knew that people suspected that Polly Frisch was crazy. They surmised that her lawyers might try to use an insanity plea to get a verdict of not guilty. The plan was to convince the jury that she had been sane when she killed her family. The only way they could do that was to find Dr. Townsend, the Hoags' family physician. The doctor, having finally been located, was brought from Michigan to testify. He was now called to the witness stand.

It is too bad they did not know the doctor's whereabouts when the trial for the murder of Henry was in progress. He had tended to Henry during his illness. His testimony would have been very enlightening. For Frances, no doctor was called until after she was dead. It was never said in the first trial for the murder of Frances who that doctor had been. We can assume it was Dr. Townsend. Otherwise, at some point, one of the other doctors would have testified to being there after Frances' death. Dr. Townsend was the only doctor from Alabama that hadn't testified at the other trials. The prosecution did not know until they found him that he had also been treating Polly for an illness.

Polly having an adverse medical condition was not brought up by either the defense or the prosecution at any of the previous four trials. This trial however, Dr. Townsend gave evidence on behalf of the People to treating Polly Frisch for a repetitive illness during the times of the murders.

The *Republican Advocate* of September 27, 1859 quoted Townsend as saying, "that he inclined to the opinion that she was then free from mental disturbance." To the dismay of the prosecution he added, according to the newspaper, "He declared this to be a mere 'preponderance of impression', and that he could not give an opinion that was satisfactory to himself." In other words, he could only give his impression, not a medical opinion that Polly Frisch appeared to be sane at the time of the murders.

The prosecution rested their case on the 5th of September. It was time for Polly's lawyers to try and defend her. It was hopeless, and they knew it. Before they even began their defense, they changed their plea. No longer would it be "not guilty" but "not guilty by reason of insanity." It was their last chance, their *only* chance, to save Polly Frisch from hanging.

According to an article printed in the *Buffalo Courier*, and reprinted in the *Republican Advocate* in the same September 27th issue, the defense argued two points at the final trial, which were printed as follows:

> First; that the proof, treating the prisoner as of sound intellect, was insufficient to warrant her conviction on the frightful and unnatural charge; second, that if she committed this and the other homicides of her children, under the circumstances insisted upon by the prosecution, she was insane, and the murder of her bright little child was without motive. On the strength of symptoms of diseases under which she was laboring in 1855 and 1856, as testified to by her family physician—such as vertigo, dizziness, fits of unconsciousness, and affection of spine extending to the lower part of the head and brain, etc., (too numerous and complicated to be even fully stated here.)

Wakeman and Bryan had said that from the beginning that they suspected some medical disturbance on her part, but the evidence pointed to her plotting out the murders. They had called in Dr. John Cotes before the first trial to evaluate Polly. Although he thought she was odd, and had found several physical ailments, he could not advise them to rely on a defense of insanity. Based on Dr. Cote's diagnosis, they had decided to not pursue the plea. It was not until they heard that Dr. Townsend was to take the stand, that they changed their mind.

On the evening of September 5th, Dr. George Cook, Superintendent of the Insane Asylum in Canandaigua, New York, was brought in to assess Polly's mental stability. He examined her closely, and spoke to Dr. Cotes who had treated Polly for the last two years. He reviewed what Dr. Townsend had said about Polly's former illnesses.

The next day, Dr. Cook testified on behalf of the defense saying, "She was then, and at the time of the alleged homicide had been suffering under disease epiliptiform in character, and that she was not a person of sound mind."

He also testified that, "The fits and convulsions, which are violent and alarming, to someone not conversant with the treatment of insane persons, would be perceived as merely hysterics."

The *Republican Advocate* in the article of the 27th printed, "Dr. George Cook ... pronounced her of unusual mind, and asserted his belief that during the period of the alleged homicides she was suffering under disease indicating epilepsy, the tendency of which is to cut out the maternal instincts." We must remember the era in which this happened, when little was known about the causes or treatment of either epilepsy or mental illness.

The insanity defense unfortunately was set up too late. The jury entered deliberations shortly after noon on Wednesday the 7th, and came back the following day at 4:00 p.m. with a verdict of guilty. Nothing would happen this time to throw the trial. It was finally over. Polly was found guilty of murder in the first degree for the death of Frances Hoag. Upon the rendition of the verdict, Judge Greene immediately sentenced the prisoner to be executed. On November 2, 1859; between 10:00 a.m. and 1:00 p.m., Polly Frisch would hang by the neck until dead.

The following was printed September 10th by the *Genesee Weekly Democrat*:

> The learned Judge briefly recapitulated the evidence in the case; told the prisoner she had every assistance by able council and the benefit of three trials on the same indictment; that she had nothing to complain of, all had been done for her that possibly could be. The Judge admonished the prisoner that she must not expect any more earthly assistance, advising her now to turn her attention to Him who is a just and righteous Judge in all cases, and prepare herself for that end which was so close at hand.

Judge Greene's speech was so moving, it brought the courtroom to tears—all except Polly. She stood there, showing no emotion—indifferent to the whole affair. It was stated in the *Republican Advocate* that during the trials, "...she maintained a placidity of demeanor unusual to those on trial for murder, and her exhibition of nerve is unparalleled almost in criminal history."

Was this final display her usual detached behavior, or numbness because of medication? It is hard to say. We found nothing in Dr. John Cote's bill to show that Polly was given any medical treatment after the 27th of August.

There was still the matter of community conscience and the concern for a person's eternal soul to take into consideration. The jurymen did not want to be responsible for having a woman put to death. Such a thing had never been done before and they did not want to be the first to do it. How could they live with themselves afterwards? What would happen when the time came for them to meet their

Maker after committing such an act as agreeing to have a woman put to death?

The public discovered the next day that the jury had attached an unusual request to their verdict of guilty. They had pleaded with the court to show Polly Frisch mercy in her punishment. The law was the law, and Judge Greene could not change this one. If a person was found guilty of murder the sentence was death. This was out of his hands. Any clemency on the matter would have to come from the governor of New York State. Before leaving the courtroom the jurymen unanimously signed a recommendation, directed to Governor Edward D. Morgan, to commute her sentence to imprisonment for life.

This was a very magnanimous gesture on the part of the jury, especially since they were all in agreement of her guilt. It was also the out that they needed. If her sentence was commuted, and she wasn't hanged, it would alleviate the burden on their conscience and soul. The majority of the citizens of the county seemed to be all for this method of solving the conflict with their religious beliefs.

The mentality of the times dictated that women were not capable of an act such as planned murder. Women had maternal instincts, which meant a woman would not kill her own child. The only explanation was she had to be insane, and if so, than she really didn't mean to do it. Their logic was that she must have had some sort of womanly fit that made her crazy and kill them. As ridiculous as it seems in this day and age, it was normal thinking back then. They had no true understanding of mental illness. Three other doctors had given their opinion which was printed in several newspapers.

Not all in the county were pleased with this attempt to save a murderess. In an excerpt from an article printed in the September 14th issue of the *LeRoy Gazette*, it was printed:

> It is a fearful thing to take human life, even to appease the offended law. But it is doubly so to allow the clearly convicted criminal to trample upon or circumvent the Law - the only safeguard of our lives, our liberty and our property. It is high time the sickly discrimination between murderers, on account of sex, be done away with. No more encouragement should be given to a woman to engage in the stealthy murder of her husband or children by poison, than to a man for a like crime. Either abolish the laws or enforce them.

Polly Frisch had been visited and medicated seven days in the month of September by Dr. Cotes. She was still waiting to hear what the governor had decided. Would she live or die? If she lived, what kind of life would it be? Where would she be going? Which was worse, death or to live out her days behind prison walls?

Governor Morgan had finally given his answer. It would be necessary to determine if Polly Frisch was insane or not—only then would he decide what her fate would be. The governor ordered Dr. Edward Hall, physician to the State Lunatic Asylum at Auburn, New York (and affiliated with the asylum at Utica, NY), to examine the prisoner and determine her sanity. The criteria being: was she insane at the time she committed the crimes? Was she insane now? If insane, was she so before, or did she become insane from the ongoing stress of multiple trials?

Figure 20. Genesee County Gibbet (above) operated similar to a gallows. However, rather than the condemned dropping, a gibbet used a counter balance. A weight connected to a rope was held by a bracket, and when released, pulled the condemned up. The Holland Land Office Museum in Batavia has an original Genesee County gibbet in a separate room from the museum collection.

Photo courtesy of the Genesee County History Department.

Dr. Hall went to Batavia as requested and spent two days, the 20th and 21st of October, with Polly Frisch to determine if she was truly insane. Her parents, Eliza and Schubel Franklin were also there at the jail on the 20th to meet with Dr. Hall. Constable Lorenzo Olcott was sent to Alabama to pick them up by order of the governor.

Once again it was a time of sadness mixed with joy. The day before, the Franklin's daughter Julia, bore her second child. On October 19, 1859 William and Julia Maybach gave birth to their daughter, Emma Amelia, another child her beloved sister Polly would never see.

It is unknown what the intention of the governor was in having the Franklins brought to Batavia. There are many possibilities. It could have been for moral support, to question them on Polly's behavior, or maybe to determine if it was hereditary. One newspaper article implied that the doctor determined that Polly's mental condition was an inheritance from her mother. It is apparent that their medical knowledge of the workings of the mind was very limited. It seemed obvious that Polly was mentally ill but they had no understanding to the true causes of such diseases.

Dr. Cotes was still treating her for her many conditions. Except for the 25th, Dr. John Cotes treated and medicated Polly from the 14th to the 30th of October. On his final bill to the county dated November 14, 1859 Dr. Cotes added a remark to the end, of which he had notarized, to protect his professional reputation.

> Genesee County Ss.
>
> ... And the said deponent further says that no visit was made to the

patient in jail but what he deemed very necessary and not without special request of the sheriff and that he seldom visited patient until and unless sent for by the sheriff and presently waited until a second messenger was sent for him.

Subscribed and sworn
To the 21. day of J.R. Cotes
Nov. 1859 before
Me A.P. Hascall
Chairman of Committee
On County Claims

Dr. Edward Hall had conferred with Dr. Townsend and Dr. Cotes as to Polly's sanity. He interviewed Polly, reviewed her medical files, spoke with her attending physicians, and reviewed the testimony presented in the five trials. Sheriff Alvin Pease, who had long been in close contact with Polly the last two years, was interviewed as to her habits and condition. Hall questioned both the prosecuting attorneys, as well as those for the defense.

Dr. Hall came to the conclusion that, yes, Polly Frisch was insane. She was insane at the time of the murders, she was insane now, and she had been for several years. Epilepsy back then was thought to be a mental illness, not one of a physical nature. The fact that epilepsy would cause someone to kill is absurd. It was a crazy diagnosis for a condition of insanity. But, they had no logical explanation for diseases of the mind.

On October 28, 1859 Dr. Edward Hall wrote Governor Morgan of his findings. He submitted a lengthy medical report, as well as a letter stating his conclusions based on his findings. The letter was printed in the *Albany Evening Journal*, and reprinted in the *Republican Advocate* of Batavia. The excerpt below is part of the letter that was written:

State Lunatic Asylum }
Auburn, Oct. 28, 1859. }

To His Excellency Governor Morgan:
Sir —

In accordance with the request of your Excellency, I have visited Polly Frisch, now confined for murder in the jail at Batavia in Genesee county, to ascertain whether she is of sound mind, and what probably was her mental condition, during the commission of her crimes, and hereby respectfully report, as follows:—

From the information thus obtained (which only a personal examination of several weeks could have made clearer) I am convinced that the prisoner, Polly Frisch, is now, and has for several years been subject to that form of insanity which is frequently the result of epileptic disease. This is now plainly apparent, and I think if attention had been called to this form of mental disease as a solution of her unnatural actions, she would have been as much an object of sympathy and pity as of horror and aversion.—

I have the honor to be, respectfully yours,
Edward Hall
Physician of the State Lunatic Asylum,
Auburn, N.Y.

The Governor anticipated what the outcome of Polly's evaluation would be, and began the paperwork. Several newspapers, local and otherwise, covered the story. On the grounds of insanity, Governor Edward D. Morgan spared Polly from hanging. The following is taken from the actual document of Polly's sentencing papers.

> STATE OF NEW YORK
> Executive Department
> Albany, Oct. 27, 1859
>
> The Secretary of State is requested to make out a Commutation for Polly Frisch, who was convicted of murder in the County of Genesee in the month of September 1859 and was sentenced to be hung on the second day of November, 1859. Her sentence is hereby commuted to imprisonment in the State Prison at Sing Sing for the Term of her natural life.
>
> E.D. Morgan

On October 31, 1859, accompanied by Sheriff Alvin Pease, Polly Frisch boarded the train at the Batavia Station. Polly left Genesee County, New York that day, never to return.

19

INTO THIN AIR

Sing Sing Prison, in Westchester County, New York, was to be the new home of Polly Frisch. It was a 130-acre facility built in 1825 using convict labor from the Auburn, New York prison. It was the only prison in New York State to house female prisoners. The male section of the prison was a building five stories high, occupying an area of 484' x 44'. There were two buildings in the west yard that contained the hospital, shops, kitchens, and the chapel. The workshops were in the east yard in another building. The female section was built circa 1835, contained 116 cells, and was managed separately from the male section of the prison.

Polly's mental condition would get progressively worse while incarcerated at Sing Sing. Towards the end of November in 1860, she still held the interest of the public in the newspapers. The matron in charge of the female prison had written a letter to Polly's attorneys, Seth Wakeman and William Bryan. The matron reported that Polly had gone totally insane. Her convulsions had returned and were very severe, and her overall health had deteriorated. Her mind wandered so that she could not recognize her attendants.

Sheriff Pease must have become attached to Polly in some way, having spent two years of his life taking care of her while she was in the jail in Batavia. He had traveled to see her, but Polly didn't recognize him either. The mental derangement that was indicated by Dr. Edward Hall had progressed as he had anticipated. They considered sending her to the Lunatic Asylum at Utica, New York.

Although it was printed in the newspapers that they were considering it, we have found no evidence that Polly was sent there. This could be due to the lack of records available for this time period. There was nothing on file at the State or Federal Archives. The decision of the New York State Department of Corrections was that the records could be somewhere in a box, tucked away, or long since disposed of. We are of the opinion that she was never sent to the asylum based on other documentation concerning her transfer to another facility.

The 1870s brought change in the way the New York State prison system operated. *Christ and the Gallows: Or, Reasons for the Abolition of Capital Punishment* by Marvin Henry Bovee, published in 1869 as a result of a public canvas conducted across New York State in the 1860, reflected the anti-capital punishment sentiment. In 1875 *The Long Island Traveler* reported in its April 29th issue, the "Ticket to Leave bill" that had recently passed the New York State Legislature. In part, each convict who was confined in a New York State prison for life had an opportunity, after 15 years of good behavior, to be released and put on probation for ten years. If they remained out of trouble for those ten years, the governor would issue a pardon. At the time, Polly was one of three female prisoners to be eligible.

In 1877, Act 172 was passed by the New York State Legislature which stated that, thereafter, women would be sent to penitentiaries instead of prisons. Section one of the act stated, "The superintendent of state prisons is hereby authorized to transfer all the female convicts confined in the state prison at Sing Sing to such penitentiary or penitentiaries as he may select. ..." The Act was passed on April 24, 1877 abolishing the female department of Sing Sing. Six of the women at Sing Sing, including Polly, were life inmates.

The following month, fifty prisoners were sent to Kings County Penitentiary, known locally as "Crow's Hill." The rest of the female prisoners were kept behind to finish a contract the prison had for the manufacture of collars for the Troy Collar and Cuff Company. Polly was one of the women whose transfer was delayed to complete the order for the collars. It was an odd coincidence. Polly had used her bandbox for storing arsenic, not her collars, and now she was making them. A sad reminder to what she had done.

Polly was transferred to Kings County Penitentiary on November 16, 1877. In the time between our first publishing and now, we found a lengthy article printed in the November 17th, four o'clock edition, of the *Brooklyn Eagle* newspaper. It in part contained a conversation between Polly Frisch and a reporter for the newspaper, an excerpt of which is below:

> At Half-past four o'clock yesterday afternoon, Detective Jackson, of Sing Sing Prison, delivered over to the custody of Deputy Warden Crummery, of Kings County Penitentiary, sixty-six female convicts, which have been transferred from Sing Sing to the Penitentiary. Mr. Jackson was in charge of the women from Sing Sing to the foot of Degraw street, and then he delivered them over to Mr. Crummery, giving this

latter gentleman a list of names, ages and sentences of the prisoners, together with their offenses. This transfer was made after it had been settled at Sing Sing not to take any more light work contracts. ...

... The women were then told to gather up their underclothing and wrap it in neat bundles, and to pack up in as small a space as possible any other little things they might have. This was done, and at one o'clock Deputy Keeper Biglin and Detective Jackson marched the six and sixty convicts down the marble steps of the slope from the female prison, round by the southerly side of the new wall which surrounds the workshops, and there they were passed over to the Leader steamer, Captain Jenks. ...

... A very quiet woman with iron gray hair, arranged in curls stood alone by herself leaning against one of the boxes. The reporter asked how long she was in for.

"I am in until the Governor pardons me out, sir."

"For life?"

"Yes, sir."

"What for?"

"I don't care to tell you that. I don't think that this is hardly the place. You'll excuse me please?"

"Certainly. How have you got along in prison?"

> "Very well. I had a nice position in Sing Sing. I was in the middle house there and had charge of the keys for the last eighteen years."
>
> "Then you are not so glad at the change?"
>
> "No." What sort of woman was the matron? [sic] "She was alright, some of these women don't like her, but they didn't obey her only when they were forced to. I did, and that's the best way to get along everywhere. Trust in God and let Him guide you and everything will be well, there would be no need of prisons if that was done."
>
> The reporter left her and ascertained from Deputy Warden Crummey that this woman was Polly Frisch, who committed murder in Genesee County in 1857, by killing her illegitimate child. She was sentenced to be hanged, but her sentence was commuted in 1859. She was one of the best women in Sing Sing. ...
>
> [Author's note: The above last paragraph is one of the few mentions we found of the death of Polly's infant sired by Matthew Bardwell.]

The transfer to Kings County Penitentiary would turn out to be a blessing for Polly. It was here that the improvement in her mental health was noted. Mr. Shevlin was the warden during the early years of Polly's incarceration at Kings County Penitentiary. He prided himself on the fact that in the years he had been in charge of the institution he only had a female prisoner flogged twice. Warden Shevlin, for the most part, did not believe in whipping the prisoners. He once had a matron severely reprimanded for doing so. Mr. J.G. Bass of the Brooklyn Home Missionary Society was the Chaplain of the penitentiary. He visited during the week, conducted prayer services on Tuesday evenings, and conducted services on Sunday afternoons. This was a progressive area of New York, which is now the borough of Brooklyn. By 1880 the penitentiary was already equipped with the modern invention known as the telephone.

In 1880 the penitentiary housed 506 inmates, 65 of them women, including Polly Frisch. Ironically, Polly's first job there would be the same profession as her first husband, Henry Hoag. Male and female prisoners were set to work in the prison shoe shop, with the women operating the sewing machines on a separate floor. The shop was run as a regular factory. Several women would be brought in from the Bay State Shoe and Leather Company to join the female inmates in running the machines. The shoe shop had three floors and an attic that was used for supplies and storage. The shoe shop was located in one of the prison buildings. The shop was 250 feet long, 40 feet wide, and about 300 feet from the male and female prison buildings. The convicts were paid forty cents a day for their labor.

Dr. Homer C. Bartlett was the physician for the Kings County Penitentiary. He had noticed over the years an improvement in the condition of Polly Frisch. Either she resigned herself to her fate or whatever illness she suffered from was finally being treated correctly, to the point that in 1882 she was given a new job in the prison. She had been incarcerated now for over twenty years, and was not the same person as when she entered. In another twist of fate, Polly's new occupation was to be a nurse in the prison hospital.

Warden Greene took over the prison in 1881. Many of the keepers had said that he was too strict a disciplinarian, and tried to run the institution on too economical a basis. The prisoners ate beef made into a stew with other vegetables for dinner five days a week. Dinner on Friday was fish and bread. Pork, beans and bread were served on the last day. Breakfast was a quart of coffee and all the bread they could eat. Lunch was a quart of tea and bread. This at the time was standard prison food.

The male prisoners revolted in 1885 for not being served hash for breakfast and expected to do a day's work with no substantial food. Eighty men were thrown in dark cells and extra guards brought in from the Brooklyn Police Department. The revolt continued for several days with howls, cheering, and cursing from the cells. The women prisoners joined in the mayhem. It was said that the screams and shrills of the 214 women were ear splitting. One would have to wonder if Polly was one of those prisoners.

The ringleader of the strike was ultimately given fifteen lashes with a cowhide whip. It was the first time Warden Greene had to whip a prisoner. He had abolished the practice and had no intention of using it again; this time he felt he had no choice in order to regain control.

So this was Polly Frisch's new life. During her years here she experienced prison revolts; crackdowns for attempted prison breaks, and working long hours every day. After being so self-absorbed this was probably the most sobering experience of her life.

In 1892 the penitentiary experienced another new governor, Warden Hayes. Polly Frisch had been diagnosed as sane now for quite some time. Oddly enough, George Bowen had recommended some years ago to have her released. The citizens of Alabama, however, had been adamantly opposed to it. Despite the passing of more than two decades, the townspeople of Alabama had not forgotten, nor forgiven, what she had done.

Times were indeed changing. Prison reform was taking a more modern stance. Many inmates were being put out in the work force rather than being kept in cells for years on end. The prisons were getting over crowded. They could no longer keep a man in jail for minor crimes or women in jail for petty theft.

Polly Frisch, now imprisoned for thirty-three years, had become old and feeble. The warden felt there was no need for this aged woman to be imprisoned any longer. Dr. Bartlett had said that he diagnosed Polly as being sane for several years now, and she had done an exemplary job as a nurse in the penitentiary's hospital. Whatever had ailed her so many years ago had disappeared. At 68-years-old she was not the same woman who had committed murder. Dr. Homer C. Bartlett informed the Governor of New York that she was now sane.

On December 9, 1892 Governor Roswell P. Flower pardoned Polly Frisch. Every local paper was covering the story. It was carried in the *Buffalo Daily Courier, The New York Times*, and sent over the wires by the *United Press*. No one had forgotten Polly Frisch, although she wished they had. She did not want any publicity; she just wanted to be left alone.

All the newspapers had reported her release and that “someone” had come to take her home. Whether this meant a relative's home, or someplace else, is unknown. The version was different from one newspaper to another. Some said friends, others said relatives. The *New York Times* printed, "Several persons of the highest respectability have undertaken to provide her with a suitable home."

It was only a conjecture where "home" would be after so many years. We don't believe anyone was left in the town of Alabama that would take her in. Thirty-six years had passed since Polly committed the murders in Alabama, New York. Many people no longer remembered.

As soon as she was released from Kings County Penitentiary, Polly Frisch faded from the public eye to become just another forgotten piece of local folklore. At the same time Polly was released a new murderess would step into the limelight to take her place. She would captivate the country's interest and become an American legend. Her name was Lizzie Borden.

EPILOGUE

Epilogue I

EVERYONE ELSE

There were many eerie coincidences in the story of Polly Frisch. Several people involved in the saga were subject to tragic or weird events. The day Henry Hoag's corpse was first dissected, there were five influential men present: Coroner Robert Baker, Dr. Holton Ganson, Dr. Nelson Horning, Dr. Samuel Bateman, and Reuben Warren—all of whom ultimately suffered a strange malady.

After researching this bit of history for so many years, we know the people involved in the story better than our own ancestors. In our quest for the facts we collected quite a lot of information. Some we felt would be of interest to genealogists who are researching the same family lines. The rest are interesting tidbits. This chapter is devoted to what happened to some of the people who played a role in the life of Polly Frisch. Oddly enough, Polly outlived many of them.

On December 9, 1892, the same day Polly was pardoned, an article appeared on another page in the same newspaper. George Bowen had been taken violently ill after returning from his brother's funeral in Attica, NY. He wouldn't recover until two weeks later. George Bowen went on to a successful political career. He served in the New York State Senate for two terms, from 1870 to1874. The district attorney died on January 21, 1921 at the age of eighty-nine years.

Polly's attorneys also did quite well for themselves. As a result of their defense skills exhibited in the Frisch case, they became notable in criminal law. Seth Wakeman and William Bryan not only became famous trial lawyers in Genesee County, they also were lifelong friends. Seth honored his partner by naming his two sons William and Bryan Wakeman.

Seth was County Treasurer in 1845 and the district attorney for Genesee County in 1851, a position he held for six years. Before the trials, in 1856 and 1857, he represented his district in the New York State Assembly. In 1867 and 1868 he was a member of the State Constitutional Convention and a member of the 42nd Congress in 1870. Seth Wakeman died January 4, 1880 after being an invalid for 5 years due to a stroke.

William Bryan had an untimely accident at the age of 45 while on a visit to Burlington, Iowa. He was riding in a carriage when the horse became spooked. In his effort to try and control the animal he was thrown from the carriage and killed. He died in October of 1867.

Coroner Robert Baker got in trouble himself in 1860 for stealing personal items off the corpses. This might explain why Henry Hoag was found wearing only his shirt after his casket was opened. Baker finally got caught while in the process of taking three half dollars, some change, a gold piece, and other items from the pocket of a dead man. He was indicted in April of 1861 for larceny and embezzlement.

Dr. Holton Ganson's life ended at the age of 65. He suffered from apoplexy, and had been a shadow of his former self for several years. The chronic seizures and damage to his brain had left him mentally and physically impaired. Dr. Ganson, of the village of Batavia, died December 1, 1875.

Dr. Nelson Horning, one of the Alabama physicians present at the exhumation, died October 28, 1880. He had accidentally poisoned himself. He hadn't been feeling well and went to his drug cabinet around 5 p.m. for a mild stimulant. He reached for something he thought was liquor, poured a small quantity, and drank it; he then saw the mistake he had made. He had taken a poisonous narcotic called aconite. He died at 7:30 p.m. after being in agony for over an hour. He is buried in the cemetery at Alabama Center.

Like Dr. Horning, Dr. Samuel C. Bateman met with sudden death due to a freak accident. On June 15, 1887, Bateman boarded an excursion train on the New York Central Railroad in Murray, Orleans County, New York. His plan was to spend the day at Niagara Falls. His eyesight was failing due to age. As the train traveled through Sanborn in Niagara County, New York, the doctor decided to pass from one car to another. Sadly, his eyes deceived him in his footing. He lost his balance, fell onto the track, and was killed instantly. Samuel Bateman's remains were sent home and buried in the Alabama Center Cemetery.

Reuben Warren, who had testified about the secret letter and was present at the exhumations, held different town offices in Alabama from 1848 to the time of his death. Many of those years he held the position of Town Clerk. The years of 1854 and 1859 he was the Town Supervisor. About the same time Polly received her sentencing, he became very ill. Reuben Warren died of dysentery on September 17, 1859 at the early age of 39.

Rosalie Hoag eventually left Chautauqua County, New York for the state of Michigan and married John Spencer Rexford. They had two children together, Edissa, born 1869; and Maude, born 1871. Maybe Rosalie's thoughts were to reunite with her brother. We believe that Albert was not interested in this a bit. Albert's descendants had no idea that Rosalie even lived. We may never know if she tried to contact Albert while she was in Michigan.

After her husband John died, Rosalie and her daughters returned to Chautauqua County to the town of Ellington where she married Meritt Thayer on April 11, 1877. They had five children. The birthdates are per the census: Ida, born 1879; Bertha, born September 1880; Lynn, born January 1884; Don, born August 1886; and Fred, birth date unknown, who died in 1887. Rosalie and her family would remain in Chautauqua County, and never returned to Alabama. She died in 1911 and her husband in 1919. Both are buried in Valley View Cemetery in Ellington along with two of their sons, Lynn and Fred.

Albert stayed in Michigan and married Ellen Victoria Stebbins on May 25, 1873 in Cedar Springs, Michigan. They had four children: Henry W., born 1874, who died in 1877 of lung fever; Bertha E., born 1876; Orin A., born 1878; and Ward Andrew, born 1887. Albert's wife died in 1927 in Grand Rapids, Michigan. Albert died in 1928 in Adrian, Lenawee County, Michigan and is buried there in Idlewild Cemetery.

Albert Hoag permanently severed any ties that he held with the town where he was born, including his sister Rosalie. The story Albert told, passed down from generation to generation, was that his mother had shot them all while he hid under the bed. Over

125 years would pass before any of Albert's descendants would find out that Rosalie had lived.

George Lester, husband of Polly's sister Betsy, died at some point unknown. Among the records of the court carriage driver we found a receipt for August 21, 1859. It stated, "To team and hearse to funeral Mrs. Lester to East Pembroke." We don't know if George Lester testified at the last trial or not. We also have no idea when he died, or where he is buried. He could not be found in any Genesee County cemetery, unless the record or stone has long since been destroyed. Was it her husband's hearse she rode in that day? It is possible he could be buried in Erie County in one of the towns near Pembroke. In any event, Betsy Lester remarried, for the third time, November 12, 1881 to George Wells.

Polly's other sister, Julia Maybach, along with her husband William Maybach became prominent citizens of their community in Clarence Center, Erie County, New York. Together they had eight children; Charles, born 1858; Emma, born 1859; Mary, born 1861; Henry, born 1863; Elizabeth, born 1870; Louisa, born 1873; William Jr., born 1875; and Herbert, born 1877.

Although Charles Maybach was born crippled, it did not affect his success. He operated a Confectionery Store on Goodrich Road in Clarence and sold candy, cigars, and tobacco. Julia's husband, William, continued his trade of harness making while in Clarence until he retired in 1888. His son Henry took over the family business and continued as a harness maker for 66 years until his death. William Maybach died March 28, 1932 at a ripe old age of 94. Julia Maybach died on March 7, 1912. Julia and William, along with several of their children, were buried in the Clarence Center Cemetery in Clarence, NY.

In 1871, Schubel Franklin bought the one half interest that Rosalie and Albert both held on the Hoag house in Alabama Center. Schubel paid $150 to each of them for their share in the property. Albert and Rosalie were living in separate areas of Michigan at the time. Both deeds were done via the mail, as neither of them traveled to New York to transfer the land. Schubel Franklin died October 29, 1878 at the age of 86 years. He is buried in the Wheatville Cemetery in the town of Alabama.

Schubel, unlike Henry, had written a will. He left an equal portion to Rosalie, the same as his other surviving children, or the grandchildren of deceased children. Albert Hoag, on the other hand, was purposely left out of his grandfather's will. It is obvious that he never forgave Albert for testifying against Polly.

It is standard procedure when a will is probated, that all known relatives be contacted, whether they are named in the will or not. Polly was still alive, however, a person who was in prison for life was considered civilly dead. In the document that lists the names of the heirs and their whereabouts it is written, "Albert Hoag and Rosalie Hoag, children of Polly Frisch, deceased."

Often what a person writes as their wishes in a will is not necessarily what happens when the estate is settled. This was one of those cases. In the end, Albert received an equal portion of Schubel Franklin's estate because he was his grandson and a rightful heir. His share was a mere twenty-two dollars. Schubel's will provided for his wife Eliza's care until her death. Much of his estate had already been spent before it was time for the devisees to receive their inheritance.

Sadly, on the 1st of May in 1879, Charles Noble filed a petition to have Eliza Franklin declared of unsound mind—in the terms of the day, a lunatic. The youngest daughter, Emily Hayes, had been taking care of Eliza up to this point. Charles named Julia Maybach as Eliza's guardian. Charles Noble, who was the husband of Schubel's sister Sarah, was also the executor of Schubel's estate. Because he handled the estate on behalf of Schubel's wife Eliza, he felt it necessary to appoint someone on her behalf. Once again an inquest would be held at the Alabama Hotel, now owned by Charles Clark, for a member of the Franklin/Hoag family.

From reading the affidavits of the inquest it did not sound like Eliza was insane, but was suffering from Alzheimer's disease. Although they were nearing the turn of the century, and some advances were made in medical science, they still did not know this illness existed.

Twenty-one jurors were called and twenty-one were picked for the jury. The inquest was held on May 6th at one o'clock in the afternoon. It was decided that Eliza Franklin was a lunatic and she was declared so on May 26, 1879. Emily continued to care for her mother, and Julia Maybach handled the financial affairs. Eliza Franklin died on September 28, 1882 at the age of 83. She is buried in the Wheatville Cemetery in the town of Alabama next to her husband.

After the mother Eliza died in 1882, Emily Hayes now widowed, moved to Yorkshire Center. According to Eliza Franklin's probate file, she took many of her family's remaining possessions along with her. Interestingly enough, on the 1900 census for

Yorkshire is George and Emily Wells, married eight years. Their ages match. We believe that Betsy died, and George married the other sister Emily in 1892.

What of Matthew Bardwell you wonder? In the fall of 1857 Matthew took his new bride, Miriam, to Michigan. Soon afterwards they moved to the Harmony/Evansville area of Rock County in the state of Wisconsin. Matthew and Miriam had two daughters: Jennie May Bargewell, born May 1, 1858; and Myrta Ellen "Kit" Bargewell, born February 11, 1860. (Matthew kept the English spelling of Bargewell, while his parents and siblings that remained in Genesee County took the American spelling of Bardwell.)

Miriam was a dressmaker, and Matthew of course remained a shoemaker, and was active in the Mason's Society as well. It is said by his descendants that he adored his girls. He was never too busy to make his daughters the latest style boots or shoes. Matthew Bargewell (Bardwell) died September 3, 1881 in Evansville, Rock County, Wisconsin. Miriam died January 27, 1920 in Minneapolis, Hennepin County, Minnesota. Matthew, Mariam, and "Kit" Bargewell are buried in Maple Hill Cemetery in Evansville. In the plot next to them is Matthew's other daughter Jennie May (Bargewell) Blakely, her husband George, and their son Edwin William.

So went the lives of the people who knew, or were close to Polly Frisch. It is ironic. Polly, who was supposed to hang in 1859, cheated fate, and outlived several of the people who played a part in the tragic events of her life.

Epilogue II

WHAT EVER HAPPENED TO POLLY FRISCH?

We of course checked all the logical places in our attempt to find Polly Frisch. Although it was highly unlikely that she went to live with her son Albert Hoag, we checked that possibility. As we thought, she did not end up there. We also checked several sources in Ellington, NY, where her daughter Rosalie lived, and found nothing. She did not end up with her sister Julia in Clarence Center either.

There would be no reason for her to come back to Alabama. Everyone she had known there had either moved or died. Since the residents of Alabama didn't want her released to begin with it is unlikely anyone there would take her anyway. Just to be sure, we checked all available records in Genesee County, as well as the cemetery records for every town. We came up with nothing. If she did not come back to Genesee County, there was only one other possible choice. Polly might have stayed in Brooklyn.

It is likely that she would have made some friends while incarcerated. Since the Minister who visited the prison was very active there, it is possible he was involved with a benevolent group. It could be that they were the "people of prominence" that were spoken of in the article printed in the *New York Times*.

Following along on this train of thought, our volunteer searched census records for Brooklyn at the Federal Archives, in all Polly's possible surnames. He came up with one very close match in the 1900 census: Mary A. Franklin, born in Vermont in September 1826. She was age 73, widowed, had five children with two left alive. She lived in a boarding house at 357 Pacific St., Brooklyn, NY. Unfortunately, we could not find out if it was she.

What if Polly had no misgivings about using her name of Frisch? We thought maybe she would try and hide by going back to one of her former names, but what if she didn't? A Mary Fritsch does appear in several years of the Brooklyn Directory—her occupation, nurse. Maybe the clues would lie in another newspaper. One of our out of the area volunteer researchers began pulling the issues of the *Brooklyn Eagle*, and found a possible answer.

The article that follows is printed in its entirety, verbatim. Our words cannot convey, better than the reporter who wrote the article, the emotion that is expressed in the account of the day Polly was released from Kings County Penitentiary.

Brooklyn Eagle
December 11, 1892

POLLY FRISCH'S PARDON
How she received the Joyful News

The Remainder of Her Life Will Be Devoted to Showing Her Gratitude to Those Who Secured Her Release — She is Now Acting as Nurse to a Sick Friend — A Cheerful Woman Despite Her Long Imprisonment.

Mary, or as she is better known, Polly Frisch, who was pardoned by Governor Flower on Friday, after thirty-five years of a life sentence for poisoning one of her children, was told the glad news yesterday, and has already begun her life out of prison by going to nurse a sick woman who had been kind to her. Foster L. Backus, who secured the pardon for her, went to the prison yesterday afternoon, and after telling the warden of his success sent one of the matrons to summon the prisoner. Although she knew that an effort was being made to get the pardon she did not expect it and said to the matron: "I suppose it is about the property which my father has left that Mr. Backus wants me."

When she entered the room where Mr. Backus was she greeted him just as she always had. For a few minutes they did talk about the property and then Mr. Backus said: "I was at Albany yesterday and spoke to the governor about a pardon for you. He seemed quite favorably inclined."

Mrs. Frisch's face brightened, but she said nothing.

"What would you say if the governor refused to pardon you?"

"I would not blame him. I hear he is a good man, and, if he refuses, it will be because he believes that I am not worthy of it," she replied.

"What would you do if he decides to pardon you?" continued Mr. Backus.

"Oh, I would thank the Lord for answering my prayers."

Mr. Backus then took out the pardon. Mrs. Frisch's eyes followed his every movement. "I have here what the governor thinks of your case in writing."

She clutched the arms of her chair and leaned forward, evidently expecting to hear good news.

"You read it, Mr. Backus. I haven't my glasses," she said.

The pardon was read aloud. Mrs. Frisch did not move during the reading, but listened as though drinking in every word. When Mr. Backus finished all she said was:

"I bless the Lord. How can I ever do enough to express my gratitude to you and to those who have worked so faithfully for me."

She then went home with Mr. Backus. During the afternoon she learned about her kind friend who was sick, and with the consent of Mr. Backus went to her house in Brooklyn to act as a nurse.

Mary Frisch is now 68 years old. She is short and slight and has beautiful gray hair, which she wears parted and drawn down smoothly to the sides. Her face is kind and gentle and was wreathed in radiant smiles of joy as she left the penitentiary. She said to a reporter that she intended to lead as private a life as she could and do as much as lay in her power to repay her friends.

At the time of the first writing of her story we were positive she did not return to Genesee County, NY. Now we are wavering a bit with that theory. Since our book was first published, we found newspaper articles that hint at her coming back to the Genesee County area. One of the articles we found contained an unusual clue. We are not sure how much of the story was colorized or fact checked by the newspaper that published it. It begins with a fairly accurate recap of the events of the murders, trials and her incarceration but contains an odd portion about a woman referred to as her daughter. Below is the portion that discusses who was there at the time of her release.

The New York Press
(New York City)
Sunday, December 11, 1892

[Background on the case in the actual article is previous to below. It also mentions how she had become to be known as Aunt Polly.]

HER CHILD CHEERED HER.

Aunt Polly had been visited at intervals in her cell by a matronly person who for some time was known to Warden Hayes only as a friend of the convict—one from the country, who came to bring a dainty now and then, and with it a broad, strong ray of sunshine to the old woman's cell. But later on it became talked about the prison that this was Aunt Polly's daughter, the only child who had escaped the mother's insane act, and who is now the wife of a Genesee farmer, as was her unfortunate mother in the years long passed away.

Somehow, Aunt Polly became known to people in Brooklyn. Someone with charity and with a heart overflowing with pity, proposed that the last days of the old woman should be passed in a free atmosphere. The movement spread; Lawyer Backus was enlisted; District Attorney Ridgeway gave his assistance, and through formal petition and personal application Governor Flower was persuaded to set the aged convict free.

FOR A FEW MORE HOURS
IN PRISON.

When the news was told to Aunt Polly yesterday she pleaded for still a few more hours in prison. It was late in the day yesterday when Mary Frisch, with her daughter and the warden and her lawyer and some prison friends—free, and some prison friends—convict, stepped into the street from the portals of the Kings County Penitentiary. The deepening gray of the last hours of day gave a somber emphasis to the scene.

The aged ex-convict looked straight before her, then up and down the street, and with a sudden sigh, she threw her

> arms about her daughter's neck and cried: "Thank God! Thank God!"

First, two siblings survived, not one. Second: Polly's only surviving daughter, Rosalie, had not lived in Genesee County since she was a child, let alone be married to a farmer there. It is more likely the alleged daughter was a friend and that prison gossip morphed the relationship into mother and daughter. It seems improbable that a woman from the rural area of western New York State would make trips to New York City to visit Polly, but it is possible. If the woman was there when Polly was released, did she bring Polly back home with her? We did find one more article that implied Polly Frisch came back to Genesee County. The mention of it was found in a Rochester, NY newspaper article about the murder trial in Batavia, Genesee County of a Lovina Egloff who also murdered her husband with poison.

> *Rochester Democrat & Chronicle*
> Monday, February 5, 1900
>
> ...The Egloff case is the second in the history of Genesee county where a woman was arrested for murder, and poison was charged as the agent. December 9, 1892, Governor Flower pardoned Polly Frisch, and the woman is now in Genesee county with friends to live out her remaining years.

The above suggests that as of 1900, she was in Genesee County. Polly would have been 75-years-old. Although we continue to look for a death record for Polly Frisch, in all her possible name combinations, until we find positive proof as to where she died and was ultimately buried we may never know for sure. We will let you decide. As more of the older records become digitized and computer indexed there is always the possibility of finding her. We sincerely hope that Polly isn't buried in one of the Potter's Fields underneath some high-rise in New York City with the record of her existence long forgotten or destroyed. We are confident that we will find her someday and have a true ending to the story of Polly Frisch.

Appendix

NAME SPELLING VARIATIONS

Some of the people portrayed in this book were found throughout our research with various name spellings. The variations are indicated below.

Bugby -Bugbee
Schubel - Shubel
Hoag - Hoage
Maybach - Mayback - Mayberry
Bardwell - Bargewell
Frisch - Fritsch - Friesch - Friesche

Bibliography

Some of the information collected to write ***Bread & Butter the Murders of Polly Frisch*** was gathered from the following locations:

Clarence Historical Museum, Clarence, NY.
Fenton Historical Society, Jamestown, NY.
Genesee County Clerk's Office, Batavia, NY.
Genesee County History Department, Batavia, NY.
Genesee County Surrogates Court, Batavia, NY.
Holland Land Office Museum, Batavia, NY.

Macomb County Clerk's Office and Probate Court, Macomb County, Michigan. Records pertaining to Albert Hoag & Lyman Hoag. Researched by Ann Faulkner; Harrison Twp., Michigan.

National Archives and Records Administration, Washington, DC., US Census (population) schedules pertaining to Polly Frisch, etal. Researched by Roger Roeseler, Arlington, VA.

New York State Archives and Records Administration, Albany, NY.

New York City Department of Records and Information Services,

Municipal Reference and Research Center, New York, NY.

Ossining Historical Society, Ossining, NY.

Richmond Memorial Library, Batavia, NY.

State University of New York at Buffalo, Medical Archives Department, Buffalo, NY.

The New York Times, newspapers pertaining to Polly (Mary) Frisch, Sing Sing Prison and Kings County Penitentiary. Researched by Roger Roeseler, Arlington, VA.

Town of Alabama Museum, Alabama, NY.

Carol Gillette, Norridge, Illinois. Family genealogy, descendant of Lyman & Elizabeth (Miller) Hoag.

Jean Brownhill; Eugene, OR. Family genealogy, descendant of Matthew and Miriam Rogers Bargewell (Bardwell).

Kathy ; Coram, NY. (Long Island). Records pertaining to Polly Franklin Hoag Frisch in Brooklyn and Manhattan, NY after December 1892, City Directories, and The Brooklyn Eagle.

Kay Batson; Wyoming, Michigan. Researching children of Henry & Polly (Franklin) Hoag.

Nancy Maybach Burkard; East Amherst, NY. Family genealogy, descendant of William & Julia (Franklin) Maybach.

BOOKS

Beers, F.W. *Gazetteer and Biographical Record and Directory of Genesee County New York 1788-1890.* Syracuse, NY: Vose Publishing Company, 1890.

Bovee, Marvin Henry. *Christ and the Gallows: Or, Reasons for the Abolition of Capital Punishment.* New York, NY: Masonic Publishing Company, 1869. Pp. 120-125.

Conant, A. G., editor. *Statures at Large of the State of New York, Containing the General Statures Passed in the Years 1875, 1876, 1877, 1878, 1879 & 1880.* Albany: Weed, Parsons and Company, 1882. Vol. X, pp. 392. Removal of female prisoners from Sing Sing. Passed April 24, 1877

Cooley, LaVerne C. *Tombstone Inscriptions From the Abandoned Cemeteries and Farm Burials of Genesee County.* Batavia, NY: Self Published, 1952.

Doty, Lockwood K. "Hon. George Bowen." *History of the Genesee Country,* collected by Chicago, IL: S.J. Clarke Publishing Co., 1925. Vol. III of IV, pp. 620-623.

French, LL.D, J.H. *Historical & Statistical Gazetteer of New York State.* Syracuse, NY: R.P. Smith Publisher, 1859 (Coverplate dated 1860).

North, Stafford E. *Our County and Its People, Descriptive and Biographical Record of Genesee County New York.* Boston: The Boston History Company, Publishers, 1890.

Pierce MD, R.V. *The People's Common Sense Medical Advisor.* World Dispensary Medical Association, 1895. Sesqui-Centennial Committee. *Alabama Sesqui-Centennial 1826-1976.* Alabama, NY: Published by the Sesqui-Centennial Committee, 1976.

Smith MD, Joseph M. *Report on the Medical Topography and Epidemics of the State of New York.* Philadelphia, PA: Collins Printer, 1860.

Wells, Mrs. Ella J. *Jewel Cook Book - Compendium of Useful Information.* Revised and enlarged by Miss Bessie R. Burton; Book of Knowledge prepared by Edwin J. Sails, Chemist. Chicago, IL: Jewel & Company Publishers, 1890.

MAGAZINE ARTICLES

Hadley MD, Geo., Professor of Chemistry and Pharmacy in the University of Buffalo. "Case of Poisoning by Arsenic, and Chemical Examination of the Stomach." *Buffalo Medical Journal and Monthly Review,* Vol. 6, No. 1, June 1850. Pp. 1-10.

Jones, Ph.D., M.D., Oliver P. Distinguished Professor. "Our First Professor of Chemistry, Pharmacy. George Hadley (1813-1877)." *The Buffalo Physician.* Winter 1974. pp. 42-45.

Dublin University Magazine. "The Doctor in the Witness Box." Based on the Medical evidence of the "Burdon slow poisoning case." *Buffalo Medical Journal and Monthly Review.* Vol. 12, No. 2, July 1856. Pp. 115-118.

BIBLIOGRAPHY

ATLAS' & MAPS

Everts. *Combination Atlas Map of Genesee County, New York 1876*, Ensign & Everts, 1876.

Stone & Stewart. *New Topographical Atlas of Genesee & Wyoming Counties, 1866.*, 1866.

"1857 Map Town of Alabama." Map Book No. 4, Map No. 355 part 1-4. Genesee County Clerk's Office.

"1854 Genesee County Wall Map." Owner, Ellen Bachorski.

"New York City & Brooklyn - 1866." A.J. Johnson, Publisher, New York, NY.

"Brooklyn and Vicinity - 1891." Rand, McNally & Co., New York, NY.

NEWSPAPERS

Batavia, NY: *Batavia Daily News*, 1892.

Batavia, NY: *Genesee County Herald & Spirit of the Times*, 1857-1860.

Batavia, NY: *Genesee (Weekly) Democrat*, 1857-1859.

Batavia, NY: *Progressive Batavian*, 1877, 1882, 1892.

Batavia, NY: *Republican Advocate*, 1857-1860.

Brooklyn, NY: *Brooklyn Eagle*, 1877, 1892.

Buffalo, NY: *Buffalo Daily Courier*, 1857-1859.

Le Roy, NY: *Le Roy Gazette*, 1857-1859, 1892.

New York, NY: T*he New York Press*, 1892.

New York, NY: *The New York Times*, 1877-1892.

Rochester, NY: *Union Sun & Advertiser*, 1857-1859.

Rochester, NY: *Democrat & Chronicle*, 1900

NEWSPAPERS, Individual articles:

Batavia, NY: *Batavia Dailey News*, June 16, 1887; July 16, 1892; December 9, 1892; December 10, 1892.

Batavia, NY: *Genesee County Herald & Spirit of the Times*, July 3, 1858; July 10, 1858; November 13, 1858; July 2, 1859; July 9, 1859; July 15, 1859; August 27, 1859; September 10, 1859; November 24, 1860.

Batavia, NY: *Genesee (Weekly) Democrat*, November 14, 1857; February 6, 1858; July 3, 1858; November 13, 1858; July 9, 1859; July 16, 1859; September 10, 1859.

Batavia, NY: *Progressive Batavian*, December 2, 1875; November 6, 1882; December 23, 1892.

Batavia, NY: *Republican Advocate*, November 17, 1857; February 2, 1858; February 16, 1858; March 16, 1858; July 6, 1858; July 13, 1858; August 24, 1858; March 22, 1859; November 1, 1859; November 16, 1858; July 12, 1859; September 6, 1859; September 13, 1859; September 27, 1859; October 4, 1859; November 1, 1859; November 17, 1859; November 20, 1860.

Brooklyn, NY: *The Brooklyn Eagle*, November 17, 1877, December 9, 1892, December 10, 1892.

Buffalo, NY: *Buffalo Daily Courier*, March 21, 1859; March 24, 1859.

Le Roy, NY: *Le Roy Gazette*, June 24, 1857 (train schedule); September 2, 1857 (weather); November 18, 1857; July 7, 1858; September

8, 1858 (weather); September 8, 1858 (jail conditions); November 17, 1858; March 23, 1859; June 27, 1859 (train schedule); July 13, 1859; July 20, 1859 "Unseasonable Frosts (1833-1859)", S. Pierson; July 27, 1859 "State Prison"; August 3, 1859 "First Appearance and Westward Progress of the Wheat Midge (1820-1850)"; September 14, 1859; November 2, 1859; December 5, 1860.New York, NY:

The New York Press, December 11, 1892.

New York, NY: *The New York Times*, October 29, 1859; December 10, 1892 "Polly Frisch Pardoned." May 22, 1877 (The closing of Sing Sing). The following pertain to Kings County Penitentiary, July 7, 1878; January 27, 1880; January 29, 1880; July 18-21, 1885; April 3, 1887; August 25, 1892; February 12, 1905; December 9, 1906.

Rochester, NY: *Democrat & Chronicle*, February 5, 1900.

Rochester, NY: *Union Sun & Advertiser*, February 3, 1858.

CENSUS RECORDS

Alabama, Genesee County, NY: 1840, 1850, 1860, 1870, 1880, 1900.

Brooklyn, Kings County, NY: 1900.

Clarence, Erie County, NY: 1900.

Ellington, Chautauqua County, NY: 1855, 1860, 1880, 1892, 1900, 1910.

Lenox, Macomb County, Michigan: 1860.

New York State Census: 1830, 1840, 1850, 1860, 1870, 1880, 1900.

Ossining, Westchester County, NY: 1870.

Sherman, Newaygo County, Michigan: 1870.

Sparta, Kent County, Michigan: 1860.

Stockton, Chautauqua County, NY: 1855, 1860.

Tyrone, Kent County, Michigan: 1860, 1870, 1880.

DEATH RECORDS

Brooklyn, NY (LDS microfilm). 1896-1898. National Archives.

Manhattan, NY (LDS microfilm). 1896-1899. National Archives.

Filkins, Abraham. Probate File, 1836: Estate Register Vol. 1, pp. 463. File Drawer No. 20. Genesee Co. Surrogates Court. Batavia, NY.

Franklin, Eliza. Probate File, 1882: Estate Register Vol. 4, pp. 157. File Drawer No.128. Genesee Co. Surrogate's Court, Batavia, NY.

Franklin, Schubel. Probate File, 1879: Estate Register Vol. 3, pp. 612. File Drawer No. 108. Genesee Co. Surrogate's Court. Batavia, NY.

Franklin, Schubel. Will: Deed Book 152 pp. 494. Genesee County Clerk's Office. Batavia, NY.

Hoag, Henry. Probate File, 1856: Estate Register Vol. 2, pp.340. File Drawer No. 46. Genesee Co. Surrogate Court. Batavia, NY.

GENESEE COUNTY RECORDS, Batavia, NY.

COURT FILES, Genesee County Clerk's Office.

Baker, Robert. Felony File: Box 3, file No. 22.

BIBLIOGRAPHY

Frisch, Polly. Felony File: Box 3, file No. 6.

CLAIMS FOR PAYMENT, GENESEE COUNTY, Genesee County History Department. 1847-1869, Box 15A.6; 1846-1867, Box Co2 (c) [308]; 1850-1869, Box 15A.1; 1850-1859, Box 15A.2.

CLAIMS FOR PAYMENT, TOWN ACCOUNTS, Genesee County History Department. 1850-1859, Box 53A.

GUARDIANSHIP FILE, Genesee County Surrogates Court. *Hoag: Albert, Eliza Jane, Frances, and Rosalie.* File Drawer No. G5General Guardian Book: Vol. 1, pp. 421. Miscellaneous Orders: Vol. 5, pp. 26. Guardianship Papers: Vol. 15, pp. 93, 94, 95. DEEDS & MORTGAGES; Genesee County Clerk's Office.

Sally Chaddock to Schubel Franklin. (Lot 77 Twp13 R3) Liber 31, pp. 172 of Deeds. Dated: May 17, 1833; Recorded: May 18, 1833.

Elijah B. & Lucy E. Ingalsbe to Schubel Franklin. (Franklin House) Liber 77, pp. 19 of Deeds. Dated: October 29, 1849; Recorded: December 15, 1849.

William S. Marcy & Lot Clark, by Attorney to Eliza & Shubael Franklin.(Farm) Liber 58, pp. 307 of Deeds. Dated: October 21, 1840; Recorded: February 8, 1841.

Shubel Franklin to Seth Wakeman & William Bryan. (Farm) Liber 54, pp. 142 of Mortgages. Dated: October 14, 1859; Recorded: October 18, 1859; Discharged: October 27, 1866.

Eliza & Schubel Franklin to Jeremiah Dame. (Farm) Liber 118, pp. 437 of Deeds. Dated: December 19, 1865; Recorded: December 26, 1865.

James & Abigail Filkins to Henry Hoag. (The Hoag family's first home.) Liber 67, pp. 231 of Deeds. Dated: May 10, 1844; Recorded: November 2, 1844.

James & Abigail Filkins to Henry Hoag. (The Hoag family's second home.)Liber 77, pp. 166 of Deeds. Dated March 19, 1849; Recorded: March 4, 1850.

Rosalie & John Spencer Rexford to Schubel Franklin. (Hoag Home) Liber 134, pp. 91of Deeds. Dated: March 21, 1871; Recorded: June 14, 1871.

Albert & Victoria Hoag to Schubel Franklin. (Hoag Home) Liber 134, pp. 176 of Deeds. Dated: September 10, 1871; Recorded: October 4, 1871.

John J. Johnson, Referee in the Action hereinafter mentioned of the first part to George D. St. John of the second part. Liber 167, pp. 378 of Deeds. Dated: August 23, 1887; Recorded: September 1, 1887. Referee appointed to settle the action of Lydia L. Stanton vs. Julia Maybach et al. Lydia initiated the action of foreclosure to sell the Hoag home in Alabama Center at public auction. This was so the revenue from the sale could be divided between the heirs of Schubel Franklin. To wit: Lydia L. Stanton, Julia Maybach, Elizabeth Wells, Emily Hays, Lodimra A. Bower, Mary E. Allen, Rosalie Thayer, Albert Hoag, Victoria Hoag, and Rosalro Guiteau.

GENESEE COUNTY CLERK'S RECORDS, MISC. Batavia, NY.

Claim for Payment, 1846-1867, Box C.2; 1850-1869, Box 15A.1; 1850-1859, Box 15A.2; 1847-1869, Box 15A.3. Genesee County History Dept.

Claim for Payment, Town Accounts, 1850-1859, Box 15A.3. Genesee County History Department.

"Declaration of Intentions.", Matthew Bardwell, July 4, 1857. (Form filled out as Bardwell, signed as Bargewell). *Aliens Declaration of Intentions,* Vol. 1, 1849-1868. Genesee County History Department.

Lunatic Papers of Eliza Franklin, 1879 -1882. Genesee County Clerk's Office.

"Oath of Citizenship.", Matthew Bargewell. July 4, 1857. *Record of Aliens,* Vol. 1, 1849-1859. Genesee County History Department.

The Minutes of Sessions,1844-1858. Genesee County Clerk's Office.

NEW YORK STATE ARCHIVES AND RECORDS ADMINISTRATION

Executive Orders for Commutation, Vol. 6; Polly Frisch, October 27, 1859.

Executive Pardons, Vol. 9, pp. 189; Frisch, December 9, 1892.

Public Papers of Governor Flower, December 9, 1892.

INTERNET SITES

Close Up Foundation, Online, Alex Jonas, Webmaster. World Wide Web: http://www.closeup.org

Author Biographies

Cindy Amrhein...

was the Historian for the town of Alabama from 1997 to 2007. She also served as a museum aide at the Holland Land Office Museum in Batavia. Cindy became fascinated with the town's history when she moved into the area in 1990.

She now lives in Wyoming County, NY where she has been the Assistant County Historian since 2007. She is a founding member and the webmaster for the Government Appointed Historians of Western New York. When she's not writing historical true crime, you can find her plotting out murder mysteries. You can contact Cindy via:

Facebook: https://www.facebook.com/HistorySleuth
Twitter: @HistorySleuth1
Writing Blog: http://historysleuth.blogspot.com/
History Blog: http://historysleuth.org/
Goodreads: https://www.goodreads.com/HistorySleuth

Ellen Lea Bachorski...

was the president of the Alabama Historical Society, and the museum director for the Town of Alabama Museum during the writing of this book. She lived in Alabama for over 15 years and operating a store called The Trading Post in the Hamlet of Basom where the authors met. Ellen currently volunteers for several not-for-profit organizations within her community and enjoys spending time with her family and friends. You can contact Ellen on her Facebook page at:

https://www.facebook.com/ellen.bachorski

Together ...

they updated the Town of Alabama's history book for the town's 175th birthday in 2001, and published a local monthly newspaper called *The Basom Post* in the early 90s. It is through their research for the newspaper they discovered the story of Polly Frisch. After five years of research, the first edition of *Bread & Butter the Murders of Polly Frisch* was published in 2001.

www.ingramcontent.com/pod-product-compliance
Lightning Source LLC
Chambersburg PA
CBHW072136090426
42739CB00013B/3206

* 9 7 8 0 9 8 9 5 5 3 3 0 8 *